UNTECHNICAL:

A MAP FOR BUILDING YOUR OWN APP

ANTHONY IAVARONE

For inquiries, contact **anthony@nerveberry.com**.

Copyright © 2017 Nerve Berry LLC.
All rights reserved.

ISBN: 1545019983
ISBN 13: 978-1545019986
Library of Congress Control Number: 2017904948

DEDICATED TO ALL THE APPS IN THE GRAVEYARD.

CONTENTS

FOREWORD
INTRODUCTION

PART ONE: THE UNAPPEALING TRUTH

1.	OVERNIGHT MILLIONS	1
2.	THE GRAVEYARD	17
3.	THE LONE GUNSLINGER	23

PART TWO: HOW TO SUCCEED ANYWAY

4.	IDEAS	31
5.	PAPER TO PIXELS	47
6.	GETTING IT DONE	55
7.	PROTECTING YOURSELF & FUNDING	71
8.	PRODUCTION	85
9.	THE FIRST VERSION	100
10.	THE NEW FRONTIER	112

ACKNOWLEDGEMENTS
NOTES

FOREWORD

This book evolved out of my personal app failure, Bistro Bash. During my reflections and research into what went wrong, I discovered that most apps suffered the same fate—why? I began reaching out to entrepreneurs, app developers, and design studios located around the United States. I discovered certain truths were repeatedly expressed by industry experts. I refer to these as the unappealing truths. They are unappealing not because they are pessimistic about apps, but the fact these truths allude first time entrepreneurs until it is too late. Apps are afforded a glamour that eludes most conventional businesses. This deceiving aura creates appealing misconceptions about apps. Understanding these unappealing truths is the first step to creating a successful app.

This book was never meant to be a step-by-step manual. Similarly, it may seem rudimentary to those with years of entrepreneurship experience or the technical know-how to build an app. My hope is *Untechnical: A Map for Building Your Own App* puts dreamers on the right track to becoming successful app entrepreneurs. By spreading these unappealing truths, the shadows throughout the app market will finally be illuminated and many people stand to benefit.

The people I interviewed for this book are sprinkled throughout the narrative. Each interviewee is featured at least once where their background and experience provides a context to the lesson being administered. Their views, opinions, and ideas are not necessarily the consensus the company they are representing holds. However, these individuals provided intelligent insight and impactful lessons that all future app entrepreneurs should take to heart.

There is not enough public attention given to app developers. Too often, the media focuses solely on their output…the apps. I wanted to provide a voice for the many developers behind some of the world's largest brands. Without their contributions, this book would not have been possible.

(Please note, companies in the business of developing apps have been highlighted.)

Thank you to these creative voices:

Andy Mack, founder and CEO, **SNAPMOBILE**

Alice Fountain, content strategist, **DOM & TOM**

Bob Hagenberg, director of business development, **ROBOSOFT TECHNOLOGIES**

Brett Mackie, managing partner of accounts strategy, **EIGHT BIT STUDIOS**

Chris Pautsch, founder and CEO, **KEYLIMETIE**

Cyrus Kiani, founder, **TOUCHZEN MEDIA**; project manager, **CITRUSBITS**

Danny Saad, vice president of engineering, **DOM & TOM**

Emanuel Kharasch, CEO, Lumalit

Greg Raiz, founder and CEO, **RAIZLABS**

Heather Brown, director of project management, **EIGHT BIT STUDIOS**; cofounder, **BUGHOUSE**

Jack Christensen, developer, **HASHROCKET**

Jake Worth, developer, **HASHROCKET**

Joe Musselman, founder and CEO, The Honor Foundation

John Ostler, cofounder, **EIGHT BIT STUDIOS**; cofounder, **BUGHOUSE**

Jonathan Reilly, marketing manager, DRYV

Kelly Graver, product designer, **SNAPMOBILE**

Kyle Henry, cofounder, Venturesome

Mandy Yoh, head of communications, ReviewTrackers

Mark Rickmeier, CEO, **TABLE XI**

Nate Schier, cofounder and director of staff, **SIDEBENCH**

Natalie Rodriguez, business development, **KEYLIMETIE**

Patrick Murphy, professor of management, DePaul University

Patrick O'Brien, founder and CEO, **LAKEVIEW LABS**

Randall Cross, founder and president, **ETHERVISION**

Shervin Delband, founder and director of U.S. operations, **ITREX GROUP**

Sterling Douglass, cofounder and CEO, Chowly

Steve Polacek, cofounder, **EIGHT BIT STUDIOS**

Vidal Ekechukwu, software engineer, **HASHROCKET**

INTRODUCTION

Congratulations; you made it here. Everybody talks about their crazy app idea that will make a billion dollars or revolutionize the world. Unfortunately for them, the furthest they get into production is merely discussing their idea. You have started preliminary research and thus taken your first step towards making your app a reality. Unfortunately for you, reading this short book is as easy as it gets.

An app can be found on several platforms, but this book pertains to applications on wireless computing devices, such as smartphones and tablets. However, you may find after reading this book that building an app is not the best way to execute your idea. For the past ten years, many entrepreneurs and dreamers have found themselves caught up in an unnecessary hype around apps.

There have been many successful apps recognized over the past ten years, but little coverage and attention devoted to discussing the failures. An app has been commonly misconstrued as a get-rich-quick gimmick—I promise you it is not. Dreaming big is important, but apps are sensationalized. Not everybody needs to be the next Mark Zuckerberg, create Snapchat, or start a revolution like Uber. Apps like AirBnB or Grubhub did not set out to be mimics of the past, they started small from a simple idea. There is no correct, or proven path to success when it comes to these intricate digital platforms. Those without technical or prior app experience are found awestruck during the entire process. This is the unappealing truth that thousands of developers over the past several years have come to realize. Too many apps are built with unproven concepts, poor goals, or no strategy. Apps are an exciting undertaking with constantly changing rules, but are no different than any other startup or business venture. By treating an app like a business, future entrepreneurs will create innovative and valuable apps for all demographics. They require, at the very least, consistent effort and time to build. It will not be easy, but it will not be nearly as hard as building an app that nobody wants.

The book is broken into two parts: "The Unappealing Truth" and "How to Succeed Anyway." "The Unappealing Truth" section lists the fundamentals and statistics an entrepreneur must accept before creating an app. It is not meant to be pessimistic, but gives readers a pragmatic snapshot of the challenges faced by app entrepreneurs. This part will test whether an individual truly wants to create an app or is just looking for a quick hit. My goal is to stop unrealistic or unneeded projects dead in their tracks while providing a stable base for entrepreneurs willing to persist. Once this blunt section concludes, readers will learn practical solutions to develop an app without technical skills. This is the "How to Succeed Anyway" half of the book. Too many projects are bogged down by bloated expectations, inadequate funding, and unneeded features. "How to Succeed Anyway" will present simple solutions and guidelines that will bolster an app's chance at success. However, I cannot promise you will succeed—that outcome rests solely on your shoulders.

There are a lot of young individuals who have the technical abilities to create their own apps, but I was not one of them. An individual with programming or design abilities can conceive an idea on the commute home and create a prototype before work the next morning. The process for entrepreneurs like myself is entirely different. We have an idea, but lack prior experience. The development process can be daunting. I first pitched Bistro Bash during winter 2013, I had no company, no funding, and not even the slightest idea on how to get there. Flash-forward to August 2014, and Bistro Bash was live on the App Store. I probably made every mistake possible along the way.

As a freshman at DePaul University in Chicago, I became fascinated with the proliferation of new apps and the continuous coverage of successful products. Most of my friends and family laughed at me when I told them about my ambitious project. I have no design or programming knowledge. Before I made Bistro Bash, I had never even set foot in an app development studio. At the time, I had no entrepreneurship experience nor did I know anybody who had ever released an app. I did not know any developers at school nor was it easy to find one elsewhere. Nevertheless, I saw the glamorous apps making headlines every day and thought I could make an app myself.

Unfortunately, I wish somebody had sat me down in 2013 and told me the complexities of putting an app together. I wrote this book to make sure entrepreneurs know what they are getting themselves into. I believe my defining trait is my will power to achieve a set goal. Once I decided I was going to make an app, I set out on an ill-fated journey to achieve that objective. Sometimes I think I wasted my best years of college chasing success that never came. There were many enjoyable moments; those mostly came before I launched Bistro Bash into the Apple App Store. I was not prepared for the near-impossible uphill battle.

Bistro Bash was built as the first of many game apps in the Bash series. I wanted Bistro Bash to be the bridge between restaurants and digital gaming. Users were prompted to find the correct ingredients of their favorite dishes before the clock hit zero. The game used words—only briefly were pictures introduced. There is one major problem with making a word game around food: there is only a finite number of dishes people are familiar with. Instead of endless gameplay, players got bored. When players or users get bored with an app, it is going to enter the graveyard quickly (we will discuss "the graveyard" in chapter 2). My original vision involved Bistro Bash featuring popular local and domestic restaurant chains' menus. Players could then exchange their points for coupons or rewards at these restaurants.

Bistro Bash was centered as a game. When the game did not catch fire in the App Store, most of those extra plans went out the window. Secondly, coupon or reward apps are likely to be dead-on-arrival. Groupon, and to a lesser degree Plenti and Belly, have a stronghold on the coupon/rewards apps. Finally, I discovered that many restaurant chains fortunate enough to build their own apps already have built-in coupon systems.

Bistro Bash was not a complete disaster. Although it made very close to nothing (nothing in the utmost literal definition of the word), it did have over a thousand downloads. Most apps don't break a few hundred once friends and family are done downloading it. There were several write-ups on Bash and some people genuinely enjoyed playing it. All the reviews were positive. I even got two name brands, Red Gold and Just Mayo, to participate (Technically, I got three, but the third was an Asian plum sauce company with no immediate name recognition). Several popular Chicago restaurants created menus for the game. Unfortunately, the gameplay was based around a simple formula with manually inputted answers, so the gameplay could naturally only be viable for a few hours. We are going to make sure you do not make the same mistakes. Success is a lousy teacher, learn from my failures.

Your fully functioning app that looks good and has no bugs will be expensive if you possess no coding ability. It cost my company $72,000 to turn an idea into an app; that was only the first version's price tag. Every feature, screen, and design in an app has its own price. It would be impossible for me to estimate the cost of your idea. My total cost amounted to nearly $115,000 when it was all said and done. Don't get discouraged at the cost—if you are determined to build your app, there are plenty of ways to get there. I started out with zero dollars just like most of you. I have tracked down app developers from across the country to root out inefficiencies plaguing the process. Remarkably, many of the same lessons were echoed by numerous developers. Starting from scratch will be a challenge, but it's not impossible. I did it, and so can you.

The path I took will be different than the one you embark on, but the major milestones will be similar. You may accomplish your milestones in a different order than I did. Many other books about building apps from scratch micromanage the details. This book is titled *Untechnical: A Map for Building Your Own App* for a reason. I show readers the major points or roadblocks encountered when building an app. Building an app is an evolving process with no concrete formula for success nor is there a definite road to failure. If you are looking for a step-by-step approach and somebody to hold your hand, then you are reading the wrong book.

This book explores the process, players, and problems associated with building an app. The chapters are not intended to be in chronological order. Feel free to jump around. Each app's development is unique and certainly not linear. Successful app stories and lessons from the industry's best minds will be juxtaposed with the narrative of my failure. It is meant to convey a practical truth that all future entrepreneurs deserve to hear before starting their app endeavor. This book does not make any promises and is solely meant to be a launching point for your app dreams.

All challenges and experiences highlighted throughout the book are relatable and relevant. Successful entrepreneurs and business leaders tackle challenges as they are encountered, and creating an app should be no different. Together, let's start your adventure lean and nimble with no expectations. What is your first challenge? Building an app.

PART ONE:
THE UNAPPEALING TRUTH

1

OVERNIGHT MILLIONS

"You're not building an app, you're building a company. Your product just happens to be an app." —Greg Raiz, founder and CEO, Raizlabs

There is no such thing as an overnight millionaire entrepreneur. Let me be blunt—if your app idea is purely a gimmick for you to "make millions" stop immediately. Money is not a good primary motivation. An app that might never make you a cent will not get you fired up in the morning. This fallacy that an app will make somebody a millionaire overnight is preposterous. Accepting the unappealing truths laid out in this chapter is important before moving forward with your app idea.

A BUSINESS

An app is a business. If you are unwilling to start a business, do not create an app. Apps require the same amount of attention given to a brick-and-mortar storefront. Treat an app like a business with an identifiable product or service, outlined goals, an execution strategy, and defined desired outcomes. To be clear, I am not saying you need to be an expert in accounting or finance or have a business background. Just be aware that releasing an app is tantamount to opening a business or running your own company. A business plan and return on investment should not be afterthoughts. Very few apps have survived on the "build now, monetize later" strategy.

Successful social media apps have created a horrible business model that too many have followed. An entrepreneur would not open a restaurant and feed all their customers for free hoping one day a continuous, unstoppable wave of paying customers will come in and order their food. Unfortunately, that is the assumed business model of too many apps.

    Have the mindset that you are starting a business and not just attempting an aspiration or hobby. Hobbies are part-time endeavors usually undertaken for leisure.

    Running your own business is hardly a part-time job nor a short endeavor. Once all the pieces are in place, building an app can be easy, but it is only half the job. Releasing and maintaining an app is the second half of the equation. A chef would not open a restaurant, prepare the food and set the tables only on the first day. No, the chef repeats the process every single day. This is where many app entrepreneurs get caught up. They do not realize it is a continuous and on-going process that needs their full attention.

THE ILLUSION

    There is a quote in the Ernest Hemingway novel *The Sun Also Rises* that describes how bankruptcy happens, but it can also apply to an app's perceived overnight success. It happens "two ways. Gradually, then suddenly."
    Many individuals do not hear about apps until they become popular companies. This creates an illusion that the app appeared overnight and the founders are now instantly wealthy. This sensationalizes apps as billion-dollar Silicon Valley fantasies. An app tearing through the nightlife culture in New York City may never see the light of day in San Francisco. Many apps fail to scale beyond their initial markets. The ones that are successfully scaled into new territories are the juggernauts we all know and love such as Facebook, Uber, and AirBnB.
    Seemingly out of nowhere, new apps upend lives and fill a need people never knew they had. These apps are accessed in mere seconds by tapping a screen. Unlike inventions and products of yesteryear, an app can enter a consumer's life almost instantly. Very rarely is an app everywhere at once upon rollout; it takes time to scale a user base. Unlike a brick-and-mortar business, we cannot physically see the hours, resources, and employees needed to achieve success. We physically see the empty storefronts of Blockbuster, but do not notice the shuttered website- or app-based

companies. All that remains of these former digital companies is a "Page Not Found Error." Therefore, we rarely hear or know about apps that went bust.

In September 2012, I was a freshman in college. I was living in Lincoln Park, a neighborhood of Chicago. This new Uber app became instantly popular on campus and everybody was using it to hail taxis. At the time, I thought Uber was an overnight success, but then I discovered Chicago was one of the few cities that had Uber. Taxi hailing from Uber had been available since April 2012. Later, I learned that Uber was launched in San Francisco during 2010 and had slowly rolled out across the country. Uber's overnight success was an illusion.

"If you want to succeed with an app, you're going to need persistence and patience. Persistence allows you to keep trying new things, experimenting, learning and iterating. Patience is knowing that success rarely happens overnight," said Steve Polacek, cofounder at Eight Bit Studios.

DEFINE SUCCESS

Success is defined differently by everyone. Even Dictionary.com lists four different definitions associated with the noun *success*. You must determine how to measure your app's success. Success can be measured by the amount of people exposed to your brand or the number of app downloads you receive. On the other hand, you may want to focus solely on monetary success. In that instance, revenue generated per user might be more appropriate.

Besides not recognizing my app as business or being aware of the illusion, I never defined success. My only goal was to return shareholders' initial investment—not exactly an inspirational goal. If defining success is a challenge, your idea may not be a viable or worthy app.

From the beginning, figure out the key performance indicators for your app to be considered a success. By the way, getting acquired quickly should not be an early metric for success.

ACQUIRE OR EMPIRE

These days, it appears everybody wants their app, website, or blog acquired. Very rarely do founders strive to continuously grow their business and build an empire. However, you cannot expect to build an app and quickly sell it off for an exuberant amount.

Patrick O'Brien is the chief executive officer of Lakeview Labs, a Chicago-based development agency that has worked with 1871, Allstate, Groupon, and Boost VC. It is a company he built from the ashes of his first app TicketScalpr. TicketScalpr allowed fans to scalp tickets on their phone before sporting events, but the first version roll out was problematic. Patrick had to shut down the app after severe cases of chargeback fraud and the use of stolen credit cards to purchase tickets. His original goal for TicketScalpr was creating an app with cool features that larger ticket or sporting companies would want to purchase. The acquisition offers never came.

"Don't focus on building features, build a business. TicketScalpr was a feature. If StubHub or another well-known ticket company bought us on launch day, they would have significantly increased their sales. Our feature would have meshed well with their products. But they didn't. Nobody offered to buy us and we just had a poor little app because we did not try to build a business," recounted O'Brien. Patrick advises aspiring entrepreneurs to solve a problem instead of making functionality. Clients will often tell Lakeview Labs they want to build a product and pitch it to a larger company. "Setting out to be acquired is a bad way to start out. I'll be upfront with people when they come to us," said Patrick. "I tell them that it just will not happen." Companies usually acquire early-stage startups for their technical expertise, or talent. Assuming your app is built by a third party, this can hinder your chance of being acquired. If your app is built by a design studio, do not expect your app and the design studio to be acquired in a packaged deal. The design studio and yourself have different goals. In most cases, you are merely paying them for their services and hence your developers have no long-term legal obligations to the app. It is unlikely a design studio will abandon its own objectives to solely work on your app in an acquisition.

A product or feature is easily replicable. More than likely, these companies can improve and scale their own features thus negating your app in the process. Many large companies have an internal development department or strong relationships with design firms. If a large company wants a feature, they can build it themselves and do not need to acquire a no-name startup. For those looking to be acquired, focus on building a business with a reputable brand or a loyal, expanding audience.

YOUR IDEA IS WORTHLESS

A common misconception among inexperienced entrepreneurs is the belief that their idea is special. They think their idea can change the world or will dramatically change the digital landscape. While its possible for an idea to change the world, an app idea is worthless.

Everybody has app ideas and most of those ideas never come to fruition. This misconception is a novice mistake and makes people overcautious about sharing it. You will never know if your idea is any good until you share it with people and hear their reactions. Stop worrying about somebody hearing your idea and running away with it to make a fortune. That simply will not happen.

Unless you have something like an actual blueprint for an interstellar spacecraft or an algorithm to predict the stock market, your idea possesses no monetary value. This mind-set will only impede your progress.

TIME COMMITMENT

Because apps are businesses and certainly not overnight projects, you must accept a long-term time commitment. You should not approach an app with a limited or finite personal timeline. Without technical experience, significant time and resources will be devoted toward getting an app produced. Not to mention, people underestimate the length of development cycles. A simple feature that appears quick to put together might take weeks or months.

Maintaining and keeping the app competitive in an overcrowded marketplace will be challenging. Once the app is released, you will need to hustle and be intuitive. It can be a grueling, lengthy process to turn your app into a successful business. If you are fortunate enough that your app is a success, there is a chance your app's value may merely exist on paper, and it may take additional time to turn those numbers on the paper into actual wealth. You are not ready to embark on this journey if you are ill-prepared to spend the next several years of your life on an app. Apps take significant time to achieve success. Over time, you may lose focus as reality sets in.

If you are creating an app, be prepared to lose your free time. Are you prepared to give up your hobbies and personal time for the idea you are preaching? Are you willing to talk about this idea for the foreseeable future to friends and strangers alike? An app can encompass your entire life—is it worth your time? Also, you already know an app will not make you instantly wealthy. There is a possibility you cannot afford to quit your job. Is your app idea worth working on after a long day on the job? These are the types of questions all potential app entrepreneurs need to ask themselves before going gung ho for an idea.

Improving your app or keeping it afloat will be expensive and time consuming. Drop your plans now if you are not prepared to spend the next few years of your life working with your app. Success will not be quick, and it may never come.

APPS ARE EXPENSIVE

A common misconception among amateur app enthusiasts is their belief an app's development is cheap. App developers consistently encounter individuals shocked by the cost of their idea. An app takes significant time to design, build, and test. If you have never worked on an app before or successfully published one, the cost of an app will startle you. Whatever you think your app idea is going to cost that number is probably wrong. If you have an app idea already, write what you believe the initial cost of development will be. Remember that number. When you have a developer scope your project and provide quotes, your number and the developer's number will be vastly different. "The number people have in their mind is just way to low," said Jack Christensen, a developer at Hashrocket. "The cost of an app is an unappealing truth to those without prior experience just pitching an idea."

    I cannot possibly claim to know the cost of your app idea, but I know this: it is more than $10,000. For whatever reason, people seem to guess in the low four figures. During January 2015, clutch.co surveyed twelve leading app-development companies on the cost of an iPhone app. Their survey found that the median cost range is between $37,913 and $171,450. If a design studio builds your app, expect to pay anywhere from $100–150 per hour. Having an app business is a tremendous responsibility with most of your assets tied up in initial development costs. You will burn through cash quickly as you develop and update your app. Unless you are fortunate enough to have a technical cofounder, paying a third party for development might be your only option to get a functioning app built.

BE REALISTIC AND HONEST WITH YOURSELF

    Your opinions and hopes should be grounded and realistic. Do not count on your app idea making you instantly wealthy. It might never even make you a cent. In 2014, *International Business Times* published "How Do You Make Money When Less Than 1% of Apps are 'Financially Successful.'" The article centers on research done by Gartner, an information technology research company. Their research was staggering. Less than 10% of all paid apps make more than $1,250 per day. Gartner then predicted that less than one percent of software apps will be considered a financial success. Be realistic with your objectives and, more importantly, with yourself. Do not burden yourself with ludicrous and obnoxious expectations.

You may make poor decisions if you have unrealistic expectations. For example, I devised almost no coherent strategy to make money with my app because I thought a restaurant or large food company would eventually buy my product or drive users to my app. I had in-app purchases, but I did not test these with enough users before release. Once the app was released, I realized nobody was using the in-app purchases. I was left with an app that had no business plan or viable way to make money. Not only that, I spent most of my funds developing the first version. This is not a situation entrepreneurs want to find themselves in.

You do not want to cut corners or base your decisions on a possible future event. Any decision you make with your app should be made using the resources or information currently available. Hopefully, your strategy and execution will benefit from taking a grounded approach. Think big, but take small, quick steps to get there. Young companies can get tripped up overestimating their resources or making decisions on hypotheticals.

FIELD OF DREAMS

Make no mistake, not every app that fails is a bad idea. Great apps that fail probably lacked a marketing strategy. Not only did they lack a marketing strategy, but they lacked a marketing budget. Nobody is going to find your app without you building an awareness and that will be all but impossible without an adequate budget.

Respectable design studios will turn people away at the door if they lack a reasonable marketing budget. If your app costs $95,000 to build and you raise $100,000, $5,000 is not a reasonable marketing budget. In fact, several design studios said the marketing budget should be double the production budget. Additionally, almost every developer I spoke to mentioned this false *Field of Dreams* misconception.

Developers always utter the famous quote from *Field of Dreams,* starring Kevin Costner: "If you build it, they will come." (Fun fact: In the movie, the real quote is "If you build it, he will come.") They use the quote to mock the marketing strategies of most apps. "There is a false understanding that if you build it, they will come," said Nate Schier, founding partner at Sidebench. This mindset will doom your app before it even gets released. Nobody cares if you have the best app in the App Store. If nobody knows about it, nobody will find it. End of story. Putting an app in any market does not create an audience. If you have a hard time defining your intended audience, it will be challenging to promote. Do not anticipate what you think people want–find out what people need. Believing your intended audience wants something is a dangerous tactic.

For nearly two years, I e-mailed restaurants and food brands pitching Bistro Bash as a tool they could use for marketing. Very few companies responded. I anticipated the food industry wanted a realistic food game, but I was wrong. An app needs to be treated as a business for multiple reasons.

Entrepreneurs should not open a business without appropriate research. This includes talking to your intended audience. The app markets are crowded and competitive, and the *Field of Dreams* days are long gone. Your app is just another among many vying for real estate on somebody's smartphone. For whatever reason, people are not quick to download random apps and your app will not be an exception to that trend.

Both Google and Apple have taken steps to make all apps more accessible, but it will be a real problem for the foreseeable future. Few people visit the second page of Google's search results. Netflix members watch the few movies or programs that show up on their home page, yet there are hundreds of other videos accessible on the platform. App markets are no different than your Netflix home page or Google search results. People rarely go searching for products they never heard of, especially apps.

THE WEALTHY TEENAGER

In 2013, Yahoo purchased Summly for $30 million from seventeen-year old Nick D'Aloisio. This teenager and his company became a major headline during the spring of 2013.

Summly was an automatic news aggregator app that attained critical acclaim shortly after its debut on the App Store. The app launched in 2011, had no monetization strategy and was downloaded only a modest number of times. Actor Ashton Kutcher was among the early investors of Summly.

Awe at the seemingly overnight rags-to-riches story and strange acquisition stipulations spurred analysts' curiosity for weeks following the deal. Yahoo shuttered Summly and stripped it of its algorithms; they wanted to create an app that delivered news of all categories in a novel way.

It was revealed that the technology powering the app was merely licensed and D'Aloisio's exact contribution to the programming was debated. The company also snagged D'Aloisio as its youngest employee. Some analysts and writers remarked that Yahoo was simply using D'Aloisio as the youthful face to showcase the old-tech giant's pivot to mobile devices and the future.

Yahoo and D'Aloisio delivered on their promise to optimize Summly's technology for Yahoo's gain. Within a year, D'Aloisio unveiled Yahoo News Digest, a clear improvement upon Summly.

Summly's fascinating success proves that each app is an evolving process with no universal concrete formula or proven trajectory. It is a notable example where the features of the app were as instrumental as the company behind it.

THE APP MARKET

"Back in 2011 or 2012, releasing an app that did something neat or interesting could get you some traction. These were apps that existed for their own sake. In 2017, there is little attention span left for these types of apps," explained Shervin Delband, director of U.S. operations at ITRex Group. The app market is no longer in its infancy. People downloading apps expect more content, high-definition graphics, a friendly user interface, and beautiful design. Your app needs to deliver across all fronts.

Even if you have the best app on the market, there is no guarantee it will ever become popular.

Additionally, App Annie, an analytics and market-data firm, estimates that the app market will exceed 284 billion downloads in 2020. These exciting numbers may appear as a fantastic opportunity, but also present a lot of white noise to overcome. The app market has been slowly creeping away from a user only looking at their phone. Virtual and augmented reality, machine learning, and the Internet of things has arrived from the pages of science fiction.

Look at the top earning-app charts. Almost all publishers with an app featured have released several apps before they found success. Most likely, their development team is packed with talent that has all been involved in the app development process before. With your sole app, you are basically going to be throwing a Hail Mary from the fifty-yard line with no time left on the clock, and no receivers open. Maybe the ball will clumsily land into your receiver's hand, but probably not. The companies churning out million-dollar hits in the App Store have most likely done it before. Publishers like Rovio, Zynga, Facebook, Electronic Arts, and King release hits in machine-like fashion. Wealthy publishers have name recognition, capital, infrastructure (servers, tech support, etc.), a marketing department, advertising dollars, and the best talent hammering away on keyboards writing code for new intellectual property (IP).

Johan Svanberg of Berg Insight, stated that "the mobile app market is highly competitive, but the economical upside can be great for the successful publishers. Like almost no other digital product, mobile apps represent a global opportunity with more or less instant worldwide distribution." Svanberg elegantly sums up the monstrosity of the app market and states the most likely beneficiary of it: successful and proven publishers.

Trying to become an overnight millionaire by yourself with a single app is going to be all but impossible. The challenge is compounded without an ability to write code or design. The idea will not transition cheaply from paper to pixels. I thought I was going to be the exception and the one who beat the odds. I wasn't.

THE STARTUP DISADVANTAGE

Most development firms I spoke to had clients that were established industry leaders, startups, and everything in between. I wanted to know some overlapping similarities a startup had with a well-known, established company. "There is one fatal flaw they both make. They have something they think is a good idea and want to try it," said Table XI CEO Mark Rickmeier. "However, the difference between a startup and an established company is that for the startup it is life or death. Large businesses can experiment and fail at something. A startup can build the wrong thing and game over; they lose." I heard this answer over and over. As a startup relying on a third-party developer, you will have one chance to build the right product. Do not rush to get an app built before validating your idea.

Besides budget, expectations are usually different. "When we are working with a startup or small company, generally the CEO or founder is working with us and making decisions," said Greg Raiz, CEO of Raizlabs. "Startups usually give developers more control, insight, authority, or the ability to impact the product." This can be a silver lining. Although your budget may put you at a disadvantage, having an experienced developer and giving them more control may be more beneficial in the long run.

DON'T TRY CODING

I understand you want to build an app, but do not attempt to learn coding solely for your idea. "It's not worth it to learn on your own how to become a competent developer to make your own app," said Kelly Graver, product designer at SnapMobile. First, time is of the essence. If you want to solve a problem, you want a product built as quickly as possible. Second, you probably have talents that are better applied elsewhere. There are multiple options for getting an app developed. Simultaneously learning design and code is not a viable or efficient use of your time. A desire to learn code is fine, but understand it may take several years to acquire the technical abilities to build your own idea.

There are numerous developers and design studios throughout the world with talent and experience. You will benefit from using a development team that has done it before. Do not underestimate your own talents. Your own talents will make meaningful contributions elsewhere.

CONTENT-DRIVEN APPS

Vidal Ekechukwu made his bones building Hottspot, an app he created after graduating from Harvard College. As a psychology major undergraduate, Vidal possessed no technical skills but wanted to make an on-campus event aggregator app. After the fervor and excitement of *The Social Network*, Vidal wanted to give programming a shot. Like most software engineers, Vidal is self-taught. Unlike mechanical engineers or electrical engineers that might require a laboratory, software engineers can teach themselves from a laptop. For Vidal, learning code was equivalent to a full-time job and it took several years for Hottspot to take shape. After numerous iterations, Vidal failed to find the success he was striving for. "Students do not attend events all that frequently to make a site with continuous repetitive usage," recounted Vidal. He discovered students usually attend events based on one-off listings or word-of-mouth, not with the suggestions of an algorithm. You cannot be blind to what your intended audience tells you. Nowadays, Vidal is a programmer at Hashrocket and uses Hottspot mainly to promote his own creative content.

Vidal and I both understand failing. Most successful entrepreneurs bombed on their first venture, but were graced with invaluable knowledge. As he pivoted Hottspot toward a social media platform, Vidal got a firsthand look at some problems associated with content-driven apps. "There is a high-threshold you need to pass for users to want to create content on your platform," explained Vidal. "If users are not getting something out of it, they are not going to use your app let alone create content for it." When people post content on social media apps, they want some validation whether that be views, likes, or comments by their friends.

Everybody uses Facebook because it's the only site where you can find most of your friends and family interacting with each other. A content-driven app like social media apps should have two things: content that people cannot access elsewhere and, more importantly, a user base you want to interact with.

YOU CANNOT START LIKE THEM

Think about your favorite app. A few probably come to mind. We know Instagram is beautiful, the featured content on Snapchat is entertaining, and Amazon is incredibly convenient to use. These apps did not start out looking like perfection, and neither will yours. Be prepared to be underwhelmed at how your app looks or functions as a first version. Do not be embarrassed if it does not sparkle or bedazzle off the screen. Your first several versions are for figuring out how people interact with your product and where it fits in the marketplace. The first version is to validate your idea, not to win design awards. Ask yourself this question: have you ever used an unappealing app solely because it looked cool? Probably not. Build an amazing product that people cannot live without, and one day your app will be beautiful.

Cyrus Kiani is a project manager at CitrusBits, a software-development team located in Los Angeles and San Francisco. CitrusBits is known for making Burger King's mobile app. Cyrus refers to popular, global apps as the Lamborghinis of the app market. "You use these apps the most and are essentially driving Lamborghinis and now you want to make your own app look like a Lamborghini. No, your app is going to be like a Honda or Toyota, but over time you will supe it up and go faster. Eventually, it can be a Lamborghini," said Cyrus. "You cannot expect a Lamborghini out the door as your first app." Accepting that your app may not be beautiful in the beginning is important to maintain personal morale.

INEXPERIENCE WITH APPS

Steve Polacek has an interesting perspective. As the cofounder of a popular Chicago design studio, Steve understands the overlapping challenges of app development and business. Because Steve is also the design principal, he encounters app entrepreneurs early in the development process. "Most people who have not made an app before have not thought about a long-term business strategy. They just have an idea and are excited about it. If you envision your app as a source of revenue, you absolutely need a strategy," said Steve. "There are no more quick shortcuts in the app market."

Rarely, are apps first to market in their respective category. A well-thought-out strategy is required. Apparently, Eight Bit Studios still gets a surprising number of people who have not thought out anything except their initial idea. "We can tell on Monday morning when somebody conceived an idea over the weekend and wants to get started immediately," said Steve. He and his team do not like to squash ideas or hopes, but attempt to nudge these entrepreneurs and their high hopes in the right direction.

I have always despised the necessity of a predetermined amount of experience needed for a job application. Therefore, I am not preaching that you need entrepreneurship or business experience to create your own app. Just be aware of your inexperience. If you have no social following or name recognition, your amateur experience will work against you. My goal is to relay as much applicable experience and advice to my readers, so they can hit the ground running or stop their unneeded projects dead in their tracks.

The Unappealing Truths:

- An app is a business.
- The perceived overnight success of apps is merely an illusion.
- A long-term time commitment is needed by the founder.
- Your app will never be acquired solely for the features.

- App development costs are often underestimated.
- The odds are against your app ever making money.
- Your app's first several iterations will not be pretty.

2

THE GRAVEYARD

The final resting place of Bistro Bash is the graveyard. Unfortunately, your app might meet the same fate. This is where apps go to die.

The graveyard refers to the countless apps that exist on the App Store, Google Play or any other app market, but are no longer being downloaded by users or updated by developers. These are the apps that were published years ago, but were left behind in the dust. The design style and operating software has changed. Apps in the graveyard look like they are in a time capsule from 2009. Publishers have gone bust or developers have abandoned these ill-fated projects.

THE PURGE

For the longest time, I thought these apps would be there forever. I was wrong. Apple announced during September 2016 that they would be purging the App Store of outdated content. Any app that crashed while launching or was no longer functional would be removed. Apps stop functioning when the developers "forget" about it and no longer provide support. Apple isn't the first company to do this either. In 2013, Google removed over 60,000 apps that were in the graveyard. These apps were purged for a myriad of reasons, but there are several likely possibilities:

- The app did not function properly, or it was full of bugs.
- The app did not generate revenue.
- Developers could no longer sustain it.
- The app had spam.

IT NEEDS TO WORK

An app will enter the graveyard quickly if it does not work as intended. If the app does not function correctly when published, users could abandon it immediately. It is imperative that when you release your app, the main features work properly. We are all aware of the tiny attention spans people have; nobody is going to wait for your app to function correctly. If the app crashes continuously or does not load, it may go straight to the graveyard. However, an app crashing because users are rushing to use it is a problem you will want to have. You just do not want an app crashing because there are too many bugs in the system. A common culprit of bugs is new features. Sometimes new features are not compatible with previous written codes. Make sure you demo your app before updates are rolled out to the public.

Remember, your app will never be completely devoid of bugs and it does not need to be pitch perfect, but the app should be functional. Your functionality does not even need to be legitimate. You can be manually inputting data behind the scenes and that is sufficient.

Bistro Bash had a lot of problems, but it always worked flawlessly. My app was not a complicated coding process, but even simple code can be messed up. Both design studios I worked with were experts at putting apps together. Before you work with a studio or developer, test out their previous projects. It does not matter what the apps do or how they look, just browse through them. If their apps do not crash, your future app probably won't either.

POPULAR PROPERTIES RULE

CNET Top Grossing iPhone Apps Ever

1. Candy Crush Saga
2. Clash of Clans
3. Pandora Radio
4. MARVEL War of Heroes

5. Hay Day
6. Kingdoms of Camelot: Battle for the North
7. The Hobbit: Kingdoms of Middle Earth
8. The Simpsons: Tapped Out
9. Minecraft: Pocket Edition
10. MLB.com at Bat

Immediately, you will recognize that six of the top ten are based on pre-existing intellectual property, or IP for short. These are official apps using real trademarks and copyrighted material; they do not need to be introduced to the public or mass markets. Most people know who the Simpsons are.

Hay Day and Clash of Clans are made by Supercell. Similarly, The Hobbit and Kingdoms of Camelot are both made by Gaea Mobile. As of January 2017, Supercell still had two apps ranked in the top ten-grossing iPhone apps in the United States per App Annie. These are studios that know how to build off their prior successes. With an unknown IP, you will have your work cut out for you. Apps built around popular properties may end up in the graveyard, but their initial success will usually keep them in the game long enough to be profitable.

SUPER MARIO FLOP

This list is from 2013, but recent consumer tastes still show a bias toward existing IP. Apple announced in 2016 that Super Mario Bros. and other classic Nintendo console games would finally be arriving on the App Store. Mobile users could opt-in for a notification alerting them the moment Super Mario Run hit the App Store. Two days before launch, twenty million iPhone users had signed up for the notification. Within a week of the app's release, the Nintendo game had reached the top of both the free and top-grossing charts on the App Store. However, Super Mario Run only had 2.5 stars after 55,000+ reviews had been submitted. The App Store's top-grossing apps during the week of Super Mario Run's release had six other games in the top-ten list.

Super Mario Run was the only app to have less than 3 stars and the only game to not have 3.5 or more stars. On December 17, the game peaked the charts of 138 countries. Before the year was over, the app had plummeted to only sixty-eight countries. If Super Mario Run had been just another game without featuring Nintendo's flagship character, it would have entered the graveyard. Without a doubt, people were playing the game to reconnect with popular characters. You most likely won't have a pop culture icon like Super Mario featured in your app so you won't be afforded that easy initial success.

OBSCURITY

Not all apps residing in The Graveyard were poor products or had internal issues. Some apps just drifted in obscurity throughout their life cycle. Large publishers dominating the market has been a known barrier-to-entry and creates frustration among developers. There are numerous articles on the Internet listing the top apps people have never heard of. It can provide a bright light on the forgotten, but fantastic apps lurking beneath the shadows.

AVOIDING THE GRAVEYARD

Do you know what is worse than not being able to create your app? Creating an expensive and time-consuming app that nobody uses.

Your app can completely avoid the fate of the graveyard with a simple move: do not build your app idea. This book is not meant to dissuade potential app entrepreneurs from developing their idea. Understanding that apps, like conventional businesses, need proper consideration will thin the herd of unneeded apps. Entrepreneurs with a firm grasp of the "apps are a business" concept will create better projects and increase their likelihood of success.

Second, you may not even need an app to implement your idea. "If your business can operate without it, do not build an app," said Jack Christensen, developer at Hashrocket. There is a false misconception that an app is required to start a business. An app may eventually be needed, but it might not be critical to the early success of your business or brand.

"An app only really makes sense when you cannot do something on your computer," explained Shervin Delband, director of U.S. operations at ITRex Group. Do the minimum you can do for people to give you money. If an app is not the minimum, explore other options. There is a misconception that every new business, especially those in the technology industry, need an app to operate. That is simply not the case. In fact, most experienced app entrepreneurs would probably fake the initial functionality of their product or service. Creating an established customer base or audience before rolling out an app may be beneficial in the long run.

Most social media sites offer free pages or tools to build a company or following. Distributing content and gauging an audience's reaction on a social media site is far cheaper and easier than building an app.

App developers will be the first to tell their clients that ideas do not need apps to become successful businesses. "The best thing you can do is save yourself the time and effort of building the wrong thing or building something that is not going to resonate," said Mark Rickmeier, CEO at Table XI.

"Buzz [to make an app] has died down to some extent, but we still get a lot of curious people. When we talk to them and hear their idea, we walk them back and ask, 'Why is this an app?' if their idea may work better on the web," explained Nate Schier, founding partner at Sidebench. "It is still easier to get somebody to visit a website than download an app. You can reach one hundred percent of your audience with a website." Broaden your mindset beyond just a focus on apps. If people who build apps for a living are telling you not to build one, they are probably right.

Unappealing Truths:

- App markets purge their libraries of old or broken apps.
- Popular properties will always make app success look easy.
- Great apps can easily become obscure in the vast app markets.
- An app may not be the best option for your business.
- Building an app is not going to make your idea a better product or service.

3

THE LONE GUNSLINGER

You will not be able to create an app all by yourself, nor should you. Excluding your developer, your company should have some other human capital. A lone gunslinger only makes sense if the entrepreneur has all the necessary skills to simultaneously build the product and operate a business. Even in a scenario such as this, there are only so many hours in a day. Time will eventually inhibit your ability to bootstrap by yourself.

TECHNICAL COFOUNDER

Although I created and conceptualized my app, I had a cofounder by my side once the app went into production. Whereas I was the one with the outlandish ideas and vision, my cofounder Alec was more pragmatic and calculated. We were a good team and able to get a few restaurants to sign up for Bistro Bash, but we were both lacking in technical skills. I have no coding or design skills. Alec had photoshop skills good enough to create promotional materials and edit designs. Unfortunately, this made little impact on the big picture: we both lacked the ability to write, read, or create new code. Designs and promotional materials are relatively easy to create and cheap to outsource, programming is not.

An app is just like any other business, yet it is still a technology company. A technology company obviously stands to benefit with a technical cofounder building the product in-house. "A technical cofounder that can build out the entire product, parts of it, or a prototype is a major advantage for getting off the ground. Even if you elect to bring on a third party at some point, having a technical cofounder to help select the right team and guide you is valuable," explained Steve Polacek, design principal and cofounder at Eight Bit Studios. "If you're making tech, bringing on a technical cofounder just makes sense."

Assuming you are the one lacking the appropriate technical skills to build an app, finding somebody with the aforementioned skills should be a priority for monetary reasons. A technical cofounder will dramatically reduce the need for initial fundraising. Sterling Douglass, Chowly cofounder and CEO, knows first-hand what it's like having a technical member of the original team. "A cofounding developer will always iterate faster. They're able to react quicker to feedback, build, and deploy new iterations without having to worry about how much something will cost." Chowly's initial team consisted of only three people. It was the first company to integrate a restaurant's point-of-sale system with online ordering platforms. In their first five months, Chowly was doubling their sales every month. The young company did not need a cent of external fundraising until their book of business became overwhelming. "I couldn't imagine receiving ten pieces of customer feedback when I'm low on funds and having to figure out how much each one will cost," explained Sterling. I can attest to Sterling's viewpoint on technical cofounders. There would always be an abundance of feedback and suggestions for Bistro Bash, but it was hard to prioritize update choices with a limited budget. A team with a technical cofounder would not need to choose one path over another— they can choose both.

It can be very frustrating to have new ideas, but no resources to implement them. This is how your app can transition to the graveyard overnight. An app in a state of stasis without updates or iterations will neither acquire nor maintain users. Initial fundraising needs will probably be miniscule or non-existent with a technical cofounder.

Sterling's perspective is also common among technical people. Cyrus Kiani, a programmer and designer, has worked for design studios and created his own app businesses. As the founder of TouchZen Media, Cyrus pairs with famous internet celebrities and builds apps for them to expand their brand. Being the technical side of the equation, Cyrus encourages a technical cofounder for their expertise. "It always helps to have programming experience as well as a designer background when you are the cofounder of a technology company," said Cyrus. "I have worked for a company with a non-technical founder, and sometimes his expectations were a little too ridiculous. Without the engineering background, some founders start to think development is a magical place where code just works perfectly and everything is seamless." I understand firsthand what Cyrus is saying. People who had never made an app before would constantly tell me new things I should try in Bistro Bash. These individuals had the slightest idea about the astronomical costs of their proposals. You do not want somebody like that on your founding team. The first version should be developed as cheap as possible.

Make no mistake, a technical cofounder is not necessary to build and roll out at an app. They will just make your life a lot easier and help your idea transition easier from paper to pixels.

ADVISORY BOARD

Before you start hiring people and going crazy with a human-resources endeavor, form an advisory board. An advisory board should be your first step toward bringing other individuals onboard. Most people do not realize the extent of their own personal and professional networks. There are people within your current network who can bring tremendous value to your own idea. The fact that you do not know any coders or developers means absolutely nothing.

An app is a business, and surely you know people who own their own business. It hardly matters the field or industry of their company. Most business owners understand troubles an entrepreneur is going to face. Any business owner will provide useful insight in some capacity. Second, search through your LinkedIn network or Facebook friends. There will undoubtedly be individuals who have experience in social media, marketing, or computer science. Talk to as many people as possible, and learn how certain things are currently being done. Also, do not shoot blindly and assume your ambition will make up for lack of experience like I did.

Before conversations with your potential advisors, prepare questions and topics relevant to their experience. Assuming you have a smartphone, record the conversation, listen to the recording afterward, and take notes. After your initial conversation, assess each person's usefulness. If you found the conversation useful, schedule your next meeting. If not, thank them, and do not plan any additional meetings.

Do not constantly reach out to your advisory board. A meeting over a cup of coffee or phone conversation every several months is a reasonable expectation.

An advisory board can make your idea or new company seem larger than it truly is. And that is a good thing. There is nothing wrong with looking bigger than you are. Try to keep the number of people in your advisory board in the single digits. Do not offer any initial compensation or benefits to your advisory board. If your project becomes successful, do not forget about them, and do what you believe is right. Finally, if possible, keep your advisory board separate from your investors. Disputes between investors will arise, and you do not want to drive a wedge between impactful relationships. If your investors abandon you, it will be nice to have an advisory board available.

JUST FRIENDS

Do not have just your friends helping you out. A big mistake I made was only approaching close friends to help me with Bistro Bash. All of them had valuable input and I trusted them, but they did not bring any supplementary skills to the table. Most of my friends had experience in accounting, finance, and marketing but very little technical experience.

If you do seek the help of your friends, approach ones who can make a meaningful impact and bring more to the table than just their input. Opinions and input are important, but your friends are going to provide that anyway. There is no need to give titles to people bringing no tangible skills to your app.

Second, you need to find people who share your passion and buy into your vision. Once people have bought into your vision, those individuals will care less about the money and more about succeeding. Just as you should have an alignment of values with your developer, a mutual passion for your product is essential for any new members of your app's team.

Remember you are going to face considerable adversity launching an app; it takes a lot of work. The moment uncommitted individuals on your team realize they won't become overnight millionaires, they will disappear. When the shit hits the fan, and it will, you need people who are going to get in the dirt with you. Hence the importance of finding people who are equally obsessive with the idea. Make no mistake, a successful app will finance itself in the long run.

HIRING

ReviewTrackers is a rapidly expanding and award-winning customer feedback platform. When I saw ReviewTrackers had secured $4 million in growth capital during 2016, they were a logical choice to discuss hiring. I asked their head of communications, Mandy Yoh, how and when they decided to hire. "There is not any sort of specific guideline to this. When we see there is a need, we will move fast," said Mandy. However, she said ReviewTrackers uses a road map to keep the company on course.

You may be surprised that your current team might already possess the relevant talent needed for new endeavors. Mandy said ReviewTrackers will look to hire experienced leaders to drive direction for the teams already in place.

Hire only when there is a need that is paramount to the success of your app. Never hire people based on what you think you will need. Do not try to predict the future. You can anticipate future scenarios, but do not waste your capital with unnecessary hires.

As the leader of a startup, you can call your own shots and determine the type of people getting hired. "Hire fast, fire faster," said Chowly CEO Sterling Douglass. "Hire people, try them out, and if it does not work get rid of them. This is the only way to figure out what you are looking for." Remember, you have no obligations to new hires and owe them nothing. Besides what is promised in their employment contract, they are not entitled to anything. Do not get sentimental about the people you bring onboard—they can be gone the next day if they do not deliver.

KEEPING UNWANTED ELEMENTS OUT

Just because somebody has an idea or suggestion for your app, does not mean they are the right fit. Be prepared to turn people away. Throughout the process from conceptualization to market, you will find that many individuals will approach you. Remember, not every person or idea will add value. Be okay with telling people no, and leave it at that. I had several individuals come at me with outlandish suggestions for Bistro Bash not realizing the cost of their proposals. Very few people understand that those features in your app do not appear overnight or without a cost.

The Unappealing Truths:

- Paying somebody to build your app might be your only option, but it certainly is not the best way to get it done.
- Apps created by companies with technical cofounders will usually have an advantage over you.

PART TWO: HOW TO SUCCEED ANYWAY

4

IDEAS

First and foremost, you need an idea. The idea will be the foundation of your app. Everybody has an app idea...*everybody*. After it became public knowledge that I created Bistro Bash, people would constantly tell me about their own app concepts. Most of the ideas I heard seemed to arrive purely from the desire to make money with no logical reason for the idea's existence.

When people tell me their ideas, I never shoot them down or fight it. Every idea is special to the creator, but the idea only has value with an applicable opportunity. Remember, app ideas are worth nothing.

Patrick O'Brien, the CEO and founder of Lakeview Labs, advises people with an app idea to go through the five Ws:

1. Why are you building this?
2. Who are you building this for?
3. What are you trying to prove with this product?
4. When do you want this product to be launched?
5. Where will users be able to find this?

Addressing these five questions allows you to think critically about your idea and get over the initial euphoria. Everybody has app ideas, but very few people walk through simple questions like these. Understanding the five Ws will also help you flush out a framework or business plan further down the road.

IDEAS AND OPPORTUNITIES

Good ideas without an opportunity are the ones that "would be cool" or "nice to have," but are not necessary to a consumer. Having a good or original idea does not justify that it should be made. Usually, the best apps today are not original at all, but are improving upon a previous product or concept. Also, your app is not original if it just takes a bunch of great features from popular apps and meshes them all together for the sake of doing so. There needs to be something binding at the center of your app.

Inability for a developer to grasp the difference between an idea and an opportunity is a leading cause of death for apps. Bistro Bash was an original idea. I do not think anybody knocked the concept nor the originality. Most apps, including some in the graveyard, are probably good ideas that lacked an opportunity. Do not build apps anticipating someone, somewhere will use them. Thinking of your users as random individuals who will stumble upon your app is a poor place to start. Hence, it is important you remember "Who are you building this for?" and find out if those people even want it.

NO JALOPIES

Professor Patrick Murphy knows a thing or two about entrepreneurship. At DePaul University, Professor Murphy achieved tenure in less than ten years and became the youngest professor to do so at the school. He has been featured in *Businessweek*, *USA Today*, and *Harvard Business Review* just to name a few. Murphy was also the winner of ChicagoInno's "50 on Fire" in the education category for his impact on Chicago's innovation economy.

He structures his undergraduate management classes into consulting groups for entrepreneurial ventures. Ventures from across the United States sign up on a wait list because demand for the class's services is so high. His innovative methods are known far beyond Chicago. Murphy is also fluent in Mandarin and leads DePaul's expansion into China.

I asked Professor Murphy how he assesses ideas. He wants to hear that entrepreneurs are readily willing and desirous about further developing their idea. "The core of that idea is going to be rock solid and changeless, but a good idea is developed to the point where it has ancillaries for further applications," said Murphy. He also likes when an entrepreneur can talk about their idea forever believing it can reflect their own core values and beliefs. Being a college professor, Murphy is undoubtedly exposed to a wide spectrum of ambition… and laziness. There are several early indicators that an entrepreneur is serious about an idea. "When entrepreneurs spend a great deal of their free time doing things that they would not otherwise do, it shows me they are onto something, and I find that impressive," said Professor Murphy. "When an idea compels one to spend all day, on the weekend, in the library or online rifling through census data or marketing databases, it tells me that it's on the cusp of becoming more than just an idea."

"The idea is half of the equation; the other half is the opportunity. For example, you may have the best boat in the world, but it is no better than a broken jalopy on the side of the road if there's no water to put the boat in," explained Murphy. "The water is the opportunity. Your idea, like the boat, must find an opportunity. There is balance between these two constructs that embeds subtle but powerful framings into the life of a growing entrepreneurial enterprise."

PASSION AND OBSESSION

Often, wealth seems to be the primary motivation behind the app ideas I hear. A desire for wealth probably will not get you in the library or out on the street doing research. Like Professor Murphy said, entrepreneurs who are on the cusp of something will change their lifestyle. You should be both passionate and obsessed with your idea. Let me be clear, I am not talking about just loving your idea. If you are obsessed with your idea, your spare time will be devoted towards cultivating and building upon it. The books you read, the content you watch, and the research you conduct will all focus around your idea. If these tasks feel like a chore and not a hobby, you need to rethink your plan.

You're already aware of the competition you will be facing and the time commitment required to make a successful app. There are countless apps powered by entrepreneurs who are both passionate and obsessed with their product. Those passionate about their ideas are going to crush you. Additionally, persistence is required to make your app successful. You may be able to fake your passion in the beginning, but persistence is not an action you can fake. Promoting and working on your app's behalf for several years without some internal fire propelling you forward will be all but impossible.

Here is one way to gauge your passion or obsession with an idea: Would you sell your idea at the first offer? Your big payday may never come; how many years are you willing to risk and stick your neck out for your "great" app idea?

SOLVE SOMETHING

Your idea should be actionable. It should make life easier or solve a certain problem. For example, if you have an idea for a social media app it needs to be more than just a copy of Facebook, Instagram, Snapchat or Twitter. If your social media idea is hard to explain or just mimics a feature of an existing app, it probably is not worth creating. Like comedian Jerry Seinfeld once said, "If you can't make it better, don't touch it."

Nate Schier is a founding partner at Sidebench, a product strategy, design, and development enterprise innovation lab. At Sidebench, Nate oversees all areas people-related and manages client relationships. A couple notable Sidebench clients include Red Bull and Pabst Blue Ribbon. He mentioned that when people off the street pitch app ideas Sidebench will often ask two questions:

- Question #1: Who are you targeting?
- Question #2: What is the problem you are trying to solve?

"A lot of people they can answer that first question, but what they are proposing might not be the best solution and don't know if their audience is even willing to pay for it," explained Nate. "Continue an open conversation with the people you want to use your app."

Your app should fill a void, fix a problem, or improve on a product already out there. When you improve on something people already use, make sure the improvement is enough to convince users to change their behavior and adopt your app. "People usually want to make something revolutionary, but just try to do something better than the way it is currently being done," said Kelly Graver, product designer at SnapMobile. Kelly Graver was not the only developer to hold this sentiment.

Chris Pautsch, CEO of KeyLimeTie, encounters a lot of individuals thinking they are going to revolutionize the world. Most of the time, the ideas are nothing spectacular. "Look at something that extends the current social media apps. Try to tap into something that is already established, and embrace a subset of that," explained Chris. "You'll likely have more success tapping into something larger than starting from scratch."

TINDER FOR X

Tinder arrived on the app scene like a bulldozer. Tinder is technically a dating app, but more widely known as an app to find hookups. It redefined dating apps and user interfaces alike. Although the Los Angeles–based company did not invent the swiping interface, it brought swiping functionality into the mainstream. For those not familiar with Tinder, users are presented with two options: swipe left or swipe right. If a user swipes right on the photo, it means they are interested in the person. Swiping left indicates there is no interest. A match is made when two people both swipe right on each other's pictures. Today, Tinder boasts on its website that more than 10 billion matches have been made and there are over 1.4 billion swipes per day.

Swiping to indicate interest became incredibly popular beyond just dating apps. A new trend called "Tinder for X" emerged. Product Hunt features a page called "There's a Tinder for everything." Here are some of the many Tinder-for-X apps currently available:

- **Flic**—Tinder for your camera roll
- **Nibbly**—Tinder for food in your area
- **Hushbook**—Tinder for unfriending people on Facebook.
- **Jobr**—Tinder for job hunting
- **Quotey**—Tinder for inspirational quotes
- **The Best Song**—Tinder for new tunes
- **HomeSwipe**—Tinder for house hunting

Fads like these pop up all the time. After Uber became a global phenomenon, "Uber for X" apps rampaged throughout the app market. Some apps such as DRYV, Postmates, and Drizly are still hot and growing, but many of these "Uber for X" apps jumped on the bandwagon without establishing a true need for their product. Try to stay away from bandwagon ideas, and do not waste your time fleshing out a "for X" app without establishing that people actually want it. Many of these "for X" apps are sitting in the graveyard.

EAT YOUR OWN DOG FOOD

It sounds disgusting, but it's a common term used among tech companies. Eat your own dog food, or dogfooding, is the practice of using the product you're making. Your idea should be for an app that you would actually use. It should also be relevant to your experience, knowledge, or interaction with potential users. For example, do not make an app that intends to make restaurants more efficient if you have never worked in the restaurant industry. If you have never worked in banking or finance, do not make a banking app. Stick with what you know, and create a product for an audience that you are familiar with. "When I look at a business plan, the first thing I will look at is how well [entrepreneurs] empathize with their customer. How well do they know them? The majority of people do not obsess enough about their customers," said venture capitalist Kyle Henry of Venturesome. "Obsession is not overstating what it takes to really solve someone's problem. Understanding potential customers' current behavior, pains, and motivations will set any early-stage company apart from the rest."

Do not build something you would not frequently use yourself. A product that the creator will not even use is probably not something other people want to use either.

CHOOSING DISTRIBUTION

It is important to perform competitive research. You may find that there are already several apps like your idea. In some cases, there may already be an app exactly like yours. The first place to start is the app market you want to release your app into. I was only able to release the app into the App Store. I chose iOS and the Apple App Store for several reasons. First, I had an iPhone so I was familiar with how apps work on the iPhone. Second, Apple is the only maker of iOS-enabled devices. In 2013, Android devices came in various sizes produced by different manufacturers. Therefore, it was quicker for my developer to build Bistro Bash on mobile iOS because all iPhones follow the same standards.

Although I chose the Apple App Store, you may discover there is a better market for your product. The main app markets are the following:

- Amazon Appstore
- Apple App Store
- Google Play
- Windows Phone Store

Your safest bets are most likely the duopoly of the App Store or Google Play. You may find your app is best-suited only for tablets or wearable tech. There are other options available and will change how an app is developed. Most developers I spoke to still prefer the iPhone first.

RESEARCH

Start your research in the market(s) you want to pursue. Before making major decisions, I advise creating large spreadsheets. Look at apps similar to your own idea. Bistro Bash was associated with food and restaurants. I would record as many food apps that I could find. After that, I recorded each app's function and if it was still active or in the graveyard. This list became a snapshot of the food app market. I wish I had done this before I built the first Bistro Bash version. Not only were food apps hardly successful, but food games were often found in the graveyard. Plenty of restaurants had their own food apps too; this minimized the potential for future collaboration. Had I dived into competitive research before my first version, my strategy undoubtedly would have changed. Remember, lack of competition or competitor failure does not mean your app will suffer the same fate. "Failures of competitors is a red flag, but competitive failure is not a red flag by itself," said Brett Mackie, managing partner at Eight Bit Studios. Find out why your competitors failed. A competing app that failed because of poor execution is not a reason to give up your app idea; however, competing apps that nobody adopted because the idea was unpopular is cause for further investigation.

Between 2013 and 2015, I actively developed at least four apps, including Bistro Bash. I always looked at ways I could expand my company and bring new apps into the fray. After several years, I believed I had the experience to release a successful app. With that being said, none of my proposed apps survived the research stage or passed my passion threshold. In the end, Bistro Bash was the only app to enter production.

I almost spawned a second Bistro Bash that revolved around mini-games or incentives that would be paired with specific restaurants. The proposed sequel had a dozen or so new features. The scope was astronomical. The research (mentioned above) related to Bistro Bash 2 stopped the project dead in its tracks.

A colleague of mine and I nearly assembled an app that would help parents set aside savings goals for their children as they grew up. It was called Kiddie Cents. The app would allow parents to establish savings goals tied to their child's birthday, holidays, or religious celebrations. Relatives or friends would then be able to deposit funds, thus ensuring kids were increasing their assets, not just their toyboxes. The idea itself was original, and it solved a real problem. Financial literacy and inadequate college savings are real issues that need addressing. My colleague and I had several meetings and phone conferences about Kiddie Cents. However, we abandoned the project—neither of us had experience in mobile banking, electronic wire transfers, or regulations. Although the research indicated there could have been an audience for this app, it became apparent this endeavor was better off in the hands of bankers. Some industries require an in-depth knowledge or real-world experience. Like I mentioned before, eat your own dogfood.

During the Fall of 2015, a friend approached me with a location-based-app idea that would sync with hardware distributed to brick-and-mortar stores. It was geared for urban areas. Unlike big box retail, local storefronts do not have the resources to build their own apps. Hence, Beep would be the perfect app. Storefronts would have purchased our Beep hardware and registered their business through Beep's website. The storefronts then would send notifications related to their business. These notifications would only be sent when an app user neared the location of the storefront. The hardware in the store, hypothetically, could have communicated to the mobile device via Bluetooth. At the time, my friend was an engineering student at the University of Illinois at Urbana-Champaign. With his technical knowledge and my app experience, this idea was probably a month away from having a hardware prototype. Three-dimensional printers would have expedited the prototyping process. Unfortunately, we quickly learned that a small Bluetooth-enabled device would not have been able to handle the traffic or continuously connect to multiple devices. Beep was beyond our capabilities and may not have been technologically viable. After the research, the initial excitement had subsided, and we both decided the time was not right. Although Beep never made it, my friend did; he has since snagged an engineering gig at Apple.

Even if you go no further, I hope you do some research regarding your app idea. Any sort of research will allow you to take a step back, take a breath, and get over the initial euphoria of your idea. If that original excitement about the idea fades, maybe it is best that you just leave it as an idea and do not waste any additional time. You will broaden your understanding of the topic at hand and might even deduce there is a better way to implement your idea than an app. Always create reports and document your findings—you will never know when it might be applicable (like if you want to write a book).

WOUNDED TADPOLE

No, I am not referring to amphibian larva. A tadpole is a slang term sometimes used to describe sailors at Basic Underwater Demolition/SEAL training. Sailors who graduate training become Navy SEALs, commonly referred to as Frogmen. Joe Musselman was forced to leave SEAL training due to severe injury and channeled his passion for naval special warfare into a non-profit startup The Honor Foundation. The Honor Foundation is a transition readiness institute exclusively for US Navy SEALs and US Special Operators.

A conversation with an elite operator became the catalyst for the idea that evolved into The Honor Foundation. Joe was shocked to learn that a senior member of the SEAL community did not even have a resume as he prepared to transition into civilian life. Joe anticipated the problem was widespread among military elite. "If he was like that, there must have been others like that too," said Musselman, "because he was looked at as an example of the Navy SEAL community." As he was putting together The Honor Foundation, Joe interviewed over two hundred SEALs across seven states in less than six months. What he learned was startling: the average SEAL held about three jobs during the first five years of his transition.

His trek across the United States was more than justified, explained Joe. "Entrepreneurs need to discover there is a widespread need, not just a one-off case." Also, make sure the problem you are solving is not just a personal itch. In August 2015, The Honor Foundation received a $2 million grant from The Navy

SEAL Foundation, the largest grant given by the non-profit. Today, The Honor Foundation successfully transitions hundreds of veterans into private sector employment. Musselman believes entrepreneurs should find an appropriate balance between researching and doing. By 2018, over six hundred Navy SEALs will have transitioned through The Honor Foundation. If Musselman had failed to react to that initial conversation, this tremendous service would have never been available for the United States' fiercest warriors.

GAME APPS

If I could do Bistro Bash all over again, there would be some tweaks to be made. However, the single largest mistake was making Bistro Bash a game app. There is little dispute that game apps can become wildly successful. In fact, mobile gaming revenue surpassed $40 billion in 2016. However, without a large social following or name recognition your game's momentum in the app market might quickly diminish after launch. Although I would not discourage you from pursuing a game idea, I would advise against it. You need to know the facts.

First, game apps can require an abundance of custom code. Custom code is time-consuming and expensive. It may require additional developers and more complex mathematics and graphics. Building a game app makes the most sense when you have a technical member on your team.

There are several apps that immediately come to mind when discussing mobile gaming: Candy Crush Saga, Pokémon Go, Clash of Clans, Words with Friends, Angry Birds…the list goes on. Here are a few game apps that became sensations.

Everybody wants the next Candy Crush Saga. In 2012, Candy Crush became synonymous with app market success. Almost five years after its initial debut, it still consistently ranks around among the top-selling apps internationally. Candy Crush is developed by King, which is owned by Activision Blizzard. Activision Blizzard is the same company that develops and publishes both Call of Duty and World of Warcraft. Therefore, you are going to be competing with the same individuals who churn out billion-dollar console franchises. Activision Blizzard, by market value, is the largest videogame company in the United States. It has the infrastructure to continuously update their content, release sequels, and create new apps. Per their 2015 annual report, Activision Blizzard owned three of the top fifteen–grossing mobile games for eight consecutive quarters. Successful publishers, such as Activision Blizzard, consistently run the table.

Clash of Clans is a textbook example why an individual without technical expertise or their own studio should stay away from game apps. Clash of Clans is developed by Supercell, a Finland-based studio. Supercell's astounding success mimics the path walked by the most famous videogame companies. Supercell was established in 2010 and manifested around the idea to create cross-platform games accessible from any device. Their funding was primarily founders' savings with a loan from the Finnish government. A year later, they released their first game, Gunshine. Gunshine was a genuine achievement, but it was not a game that Supercell could bank their future on. On their website, Supercell declared they wanted to build games "people will play for years."

Supercell discovered that most players got bored playing Gunshine after a couple months; the development team went back to the drawing board. The studio decided to cease focus on delivering content accessible from multiple devices and instead start building apps for tablets. By 2012, Supercell had developed several games and projects that led to their crown jewel: Clash of Clans. Learning from prior mistakes and taking advantage of the new tablet market, Supercell developed a hit game that had mass-market appeal. Today, Supercell has offices in Helsinki, San Francisco, Tokyo, Seoul, and Beijing. Game studios such as Supercell find success after learning from the mistakes made during earlier projects.

On the other hand, there have been some unique lone-gunslinger success stories. The strange but nonetheless fascinating story of Dong Nguyen validates that a single individual can have runaway success in the game-app market. Dong is an experienced programmer from Vietnam. By sixteen, Dong was programming his own games and was one of the top-twenty programmers at his university in Vietnam. Dong noticed that individuals like to play games using only one hand and began building games built around tapping, an easy movement for a single hand. He created a game with designs that mimicked Nintendo's Super Mario Bros. The players, by tapping the screen, had to navigate a pixelated bird through green pipes. Flappy Bird was born.

Remarkably, Dong only tweeted marketing material once about Flappy Bird. It was not until months later that users, frustrated with how challenging a simple game could be, helped the game go viral. Although the game was rudimentary and simple, most players could not last more than a few seconds before their pixelated bird crashed. Players angrily tweeted, posted, and became vocal about Flappy Bird. The game eventually topped both the App Store and Google Play, Dong was earning an estimated $50,000 per day, and its success became a pop-culture sensation. Users directed fury and hatred toward the "evil" creator, and Dong was overwhelmed. He took Flappy Bird off the market at the peak of its popularity.

Not surprisingly, Flappy Bird was an original inspiration of mine. A single man created one of the most successful mobile games on the planet using simple mechanics and graphics, but I overlooked a crucial factor in Flappy Bird's success: the expertise and experience of Dong.

DISRUPTION

John Ostler is a self-proclaimed lover of toys, a seasoned entrepreneur and one of the brightest individuals I have encountered in the Chicago tech scene. John is a bubbling caldron of fascinating ideas and an expert on user experience (UX). He is cofounder of Eight Bit Studios, a Chicago design studio that ascended into Inc.'s 5000 List of Fastest Growing Private Companies in the United States during 2016. John and his cofounders have fended off takeover offers for several years to maintain their quirky company culture and innovation.

I asked John if a non-technical startup could successfully bootstrap an app. John believes a budget can dampen creativity, but it only becomes a significant problem in the case of disruption. "It all depends on how disruptive you are trying to be. Advertising and marketing expenses can be cost-prohibitive if you are trying to disrupt a billion-dollar oversaturated market," said John. "Parking spot apps are a good example of an idea that was not intended to be disruptive. Companies acquired several parking spots and built a simple WordPress app for consumers to reserve those spots. They began small and slowly accumulated enough capital and clout to become disruptive. In the beginning, a few random parking spaces was not enough to disrupt the entire parking garage industry."

    Do not plan on disrupting the market without a sizeable budget to punch your way in. Consumers will not just stumble upon your "disruptive" app. "The only time people go browsing through the App Store looking for new apps is if it's their first iPhone…and they are thirteen," joked Ostler. Convincing users to change their daily behaviors and leave their favorite app to join yours will not happen without a strong marketing strategy.

Going back to game apps, John does not believe game apps can be disruptive. Along with cofounding Eight Bit Studios, John is also the cofounder and "chief mad scientist" of Bughouse. Bughouse aims to create the next generation of children's books, apps, toys, and games. John believes the only threshold popular games need to pass is the fun factor. "Games are way different than regular apps. Finding the fun is the hardest part. A lot of top companies searching for new products to invest in their motto is 'find the fun' whether it's a toy, a board game, or a digital game." I can affirm John's statements. Bistro Bash was a good game and the mechanics worked, but I am not sure it was wholesome, contagious fun. Maintaining a players' interest over an extended period is challenging as tastes change and new games enter the market.

He thinks people are too quick to use disruption as a marketing strategy. "Many times, entrepreneurs will not acknowledge an industry has already been disrupted. If an entrepreneur cites other apps that are already disrupting the targeted industry, then the disruption is done," explained John. Although he admits disruption is possible, John advises startups to stay away from using disruption as a tactic. "If somebody asks you: 'Couldn't I just do that with (fill in the blank)?' in response to your pitched idea, that is an early indicator of a shaky concept."

ZERO TO ONE DISRUPTION

Billionaire Peter Thiel's well-known book *Zero to One* is a terrific read for aspiring entrepreneurs looking to make the next billion-dollar startup. As a cofounder of PayPal and Facebook board member, Thiel has been a disruptor all his life. He's also been an early investor in a plethora of other companies including: SpaceX, Stripe, Yelp, Palantir Technologies, LinkedIn, and Xero. In his book, Thiel attacks the overuse of the word *disruption*. He says that disruption is used as a "buzzword for anything posing as trendy and new." It can also invite hostilities. If the focus of your app is to disrupt other apps, you are identifying yourself as a threat. Labeling yourself as disruptive will grab unwanted attention and you may not have the capital to fend off attacks from larger companies. Secondly, Thiel believes those who say they are disrupters "see themselves through older firms' eyes." Instead of focusing on competing with another product and being disruptive, focus on your own technology and value.

How to Succeed:

- Don't just brainstorm ways to get rich.
- Stay away from "nice to have" app ideas.
- Original ideas do not necessarily make good apps.
- Entrepreneurs with a passion for their app will always have a better shot at success. Stick with industries you are familiar with and ideas that you have a passion for.

- First, make sure the problem you are solving is not just a personal itch. Second, make sure your solution is something people would actually use.
- Research all aspects of your idea.
- Stay away from game apps if you lack technical expertise (design, programming, etc.).
- The word *disruption* should not be mentioned in your pitch.

5

PAPER TO PIXELS

Based on your research, you will know whether to proceed or stop pre-production on your idea. If you choose to move ahead, you should attempt to proof your concept before bringing it to a developer. Not only is idea validation important to the success of your future app, but most respected developers will be encouraged that you attempted a prototype. You do not need to validate every feature and nook in your future app. You need to start with the first feature, the problem you are solving or the main benefit your app will be providing.

READY, FIRE, AIM

Ready, fire, aim. Serial entrepreneurs, academia, and industry pioneers often blurt this overused quote. They advise individuals to forget about strategy or market research and just innovate. Acting seems to be the hardest step for a lot of people. Dreamers get too caught up in perfecting their vision, overthinking, and planning, but they never act. Hence, ready, fire, aim.

This was my approach when originally assembling Bistro Bash. Within hours of conceiving the idea, I had already drawn out the entire wireframe with markers and colored pencils. Within a month, my friend created graphic design work and I found a lawyer for a nondisclosure agreement, formed a limited liability company, and began searching for a developer. After a month of searching, I found a freelancing developer. During this time, I did very little research or strategizing. I knew little about other apps in my category and never spoke to a single professional app developer. I focused on fleshing out the idea and sketching possible screens on scratch paper; however, there was a lot of start and stop. My inexperienced, first-time developer never wrote a line of code and hardly returned my calls. The project idled for months. I had already spent several thousand dollars and had nothing to show for it. Not to mention, I had not even mimicked the user experience of the gameplay. I was merely trying to build an app that hypothetically might have been fun. These were all amateur mistakes. For example, finding an attorney should have been the last thing on my mind.

The ready-fire-aim process got me on the path to finally develop Bistro Bash, but having no technical skill slowed it down. Had I been proficient in design or had I known how to write code, I would have been hammering out programs and designs around the clock. Without a technical skill, "ready, fire, aim" is not always a convenient or cost-effective approach in the beginning.

Eventually, I restructured my limited liability company to allow for external financing. I was then able to raise sufficient capital to work with a professional development studio. Before you start spending money and wasting time, do your research and talk with people who have made apps or started a business before. You should not immediately be contacting developers or lawyers. Work on your idea, mimic the user experience, and proof your concept.

When your app or a demo of your product is available, "ready, fire, aim" should become your mantra. Go out there, attack the market with your product, and leave no stone unturned or opportunity unexplored.

AVOID SECRECY

We have already established nobody is going to steal your idea. Do yourself a favor and get over this irrational fear. You need to find out what other people objectively think about your idea. "The first thing someone with an app idea should do is tell everyone they know and get feedback. Too many people think secrecy is critical to a great app idea. The best thing someone can do is get feedback and improve the concept," said Andy Mack, CEO of SnapMobile.

Feedback is important, but people's initial reaction and facial expressions will be just as telling. Initially, do not be concerned about explaining how your app will work, but explain what your app will do. "Oftentimes, people who make stuff go into a bubble, and they have certain beliefs or assumptions. It is important to show it to people who are not closely tied to the project to get feedback," said Steve Polacek, cofounder at Eight Bit Studios.

Get over your ego and forget your shortcomings. Try to speak to as many people about your idea and get challenged by as many critics as possible. This is the only way to start and the first step to learning about your app.

BASIC VISUALS

Start by sketching your idea on scratch paper. It does not have to be fancy, but you should start visualizing how the idea will look or function. There are no advanced drawing skills required—just be simple. In fact, if you search online for "[insert tablet or phone name] template screen" you will find printable screens to draw on. For example, if you type "iPhone 7 template screen" you will get outlines of an iPhone 7 that you can print, make copies of, and start drawing on. Worry less about the design and colors, and focus on functionality and how the user will interact with your app.

BE BRIGHT

Manny Kharasch knows all too well that sometimes an idea can just hit you. In his case, it literally hit him. While jogging on a dimly lit street at night, Manny was struck by a car. Because of homework and a busy schedule, Manny had no choice but to run at night. "I was actually wearing a reflective garment, but the problem with reflective technology: it requires a light source. Unfortunately, the car that hit me didn't have headlights on, nor were there streetlights," explained Manny. "Reflective technology is really effective, but you need a light source for it to work."

Naturally, a lightbulb went off in his head. Although he thinks it sounds cheesy, the inspiration for his product was pure. Manny wanted to make a product that made somebody the light source. At seventeen years old, Manny got to work on a prototype almost immediately. As a proof of concept, he used parts he bought from RadioShack and Amazon. He soldered a battery and LED strip together. Evidently, a lifelong passion for electronics had paid off.

After proving the concept was viable, Manny had two hurdles to overcome: find an LED and garment manufacturer. He was fortunate to intrigue the owner of RemPhos Technologies, a high-tech LED manufacturer. I was stunned listening to his story and asked him how he found these companies. Manny grinned. "Elbow grease," he said. He just Googled "LED Manufacturers" and filled out the contact boxes for more than thirty companies. After pitching his idea and providing proof of concept, RemPhos bought in. Lumalit was formed, and Manny was named the chief executive officer. Now, they only needed to make the garment.

Lumalit eventually discovered a lady located in New York. Together, they created a Frankenstein jacket made of multiple popular coats sewn together. Manny took the best features from each. From this Frankenstein prototype, they constructed a garment pattern—a universal blueprint that any clothing manufacturer would understand.

Although not an app, Manny refers to his jacket as wearable technology. Like an app, his jacket had never been attempted before and needed a proof of concept. With determination and the right idea, you too can create a Frankenstein prototype. Testing user experience and validating the main value of your product is essential.

MIMIC THE USER EXPERIENCE

"You do not need a full app to test something," said Kyle Henry, former chief marketing officer of Tide Spin and venture capitalist. "Mimic the behavior or feature that you want in your app. Obviously, you cannot scale the product if the feature is being faked, but you can still find out how customers react." Forget for a moment that you are building an app, and focus on what that app will be doing. Break down that main feature, and innovate from there.

Eight Bit Studios mentioned there was once an individual with an app idea with no technical experience but was extremely savvy with Microsoft PowerPoint. He mimicked the user experience of his app idea in PowerPoint and tested the idea repeatedly. "Go back and think about how people used to invent stuff. Just get a napkin out and put some wires or gears in an illustration," said John Ostler, cofounder of Eight Bit Studios. "I like anybody who is willing to come in with a sketch of their idea. It shows they are interested in getting muddy to show the user experience versus someone who just sits, talks, and rifles off features."

Before I made Bistro Bash, I used slips of paper to mimic the gameplay screen. In Bistro Bash, users were prompted to find the correct ingredients among wrong answers. I simply laid out twelve slips of paper, and people tried to find the three correct answers in less than ten seconds.

Some developers I spoke to advocated just going out on the street or in a coffee shop and asking people their opinions. Show them your sketches, rudimentary prototypes, or whatever else your creative mind cooks up.

SCREENSHOTS

Besides sketching and other conventional designs, Patrick O'Brien, the founder of Lakeview Labs, rarely entertains app-idea submissions without accompanying visuals.

"It is a waste of time at this point. If a person is just pitching us on an idea, there is a slim chance we will work on that. On the other hand, a conversation is warranted if they have done their research or at least attempted to draw out their wireframes," explained Patrick. Sketches are nice, but he says a client should showcase examples. "I like when clients just take screenshots of their favorite app and mesh it all together." Everybody has their favorite design or functionality in an app. Instead of creating your own wireframes, focus on screenshotting app features that mimic what you want in your own app. For example, maybe you want your sign-in page to look like Facebook, the menu to mimic Uber's, or the user profile inspired by LinkedIn.

Screenshots are simple and can provide great insight into your thinking and vision. When your app gets built, the developer will at least have a foundation for inspiration.

Remember that your app cannot possibly look as stylish as your favorite apps, so do not expect exact replicas!

LOGO

I know a logo makes a project feel real, but it should not be an immediate priority. First, your title or branding will probably change before your app is released. Second, a logo can put unneeded stress on your developer to match the logo's branding. Third, do not waste your money. Yes, getting a logo from a crowdsourced website can be cheap but not necessarily worth the savings. Your company or idea will not be taken any more seriously with a logo attached. In fact, most developers, especially design studios, prefer you come to them with as little branding as possible. The designs you have may not be compatible with new technology or be relevant after going through the production process. Focus on your idea and concept, not a logo or premature professional designs.

IMPOSE YOUR IDEA

Cyrus Kiani, a project manager at CitrusBits, is also the founder of TouchZen Media. TouchZen is a software development and design company specializing in iOS and Android applications. They build mobile applications for well-known and emerging brands. "Most people do not understand that marketing is a huge part of it. There are a lot of great apps in the store that are well designed, well developed, and perfect in every way that never go anywhere because there is no plan to market," said Cyrus. "I did not have marketing abilities or any funding for marketing, but I could develop apps." Cyrus began approaching Instagram users with over 100,000 followers or YouTube channels with more than 200,000 subscribers.

The first app TouchZen made was with Yovanna "Rawvana" Mendoza, a YouTube chef specializing in raw vegan recipes. Together, Yovanna and Cyrus released Rawvana's Raw Recipes on iOS. It garnered over three hundred five-star reviews and reached top place in the food-and-drink category for two months in 2014. Not only that, but it reached the top–two hundred overall apps on the App Store at one point. If Cyrus had made a recipe app by himself, it would have probably stumbled into the graveyard. With no name recognition or marketing budget, it would have been challenging for Cyrus to push a food-and-drink app. By tapping into a popular channel that had yet to breach the app market, Cyrus established a lucrative app. Since Rawvana's Raw Recipes was released, TouchZen has released three more apps to reach the number-one spot in the food-and-drink category on the App Store. They never spent a dime on marketing. It is easier to tap into an existing marketing channel than to create your own. Find out if there are individuals with a large audience that overlaps with your intended users. Maybe you can team up and impose your idea over their existing brand. It may seem unlikely that an Internet celebrity would agree to your idea, but it never hurts to ask.

TALK TO BUSINESSES

There are a variety of ways to get businesses interested in your app before it is even built. Speak to small businesses in your area and gauge their interest. If possible, see if you can get a letter of intent. A letter of intent is a simple agreement that outlines terms before an official contract is signed. Although the letter of intent is not binding, it may help you snowball that into further engagements with other businesses. "If you do not have businesses in your own area or network interested in your product, there is a slim chance you are going to find others to pay for it," said Kelly Graver, a product designer at SnapMobile. Speaking to businesses early may save you from making a product nobody wants.

It will be beneficial to not only test your idea with future users but also with the businesses or individuals that could help make your service lucrative.

How to Succeed:

- A lack of technical experience doesn't mean you cannot validate your idea through other creative means.
- Tell as many people and businesses as possible about your idea. You must get feedback!
- Do not waste money on pointless things, like a logo, until you have validated your idea.
- If possible, try to impose your brands on existing channels to increase your chances at success.

6

GETTING IT DONE

Finding a developer is easy. Finding a credible and trustworthy developer is tricky. Unless you have a technical cofounder, you are left with two main choices: a freelancing developer or a design studio. Approach developers with a product brief, a vision, an explanation of why you want to build the app, and a description of who your users will be. Let the developing companies guide you, and avoid micromanaging their work. They have done this before.

Before you raise capital, it is important to get a project scope. A project scope breaks down your app's production goals and their associated costs. These scopes will determine your eventual fundraising needs. Usually, the initial scope will examine all potential features you expect your app to have. This will produce a bloated and unrealistic price. Once you separate the needed or essentials features from the wanted but unneeded features, the cost will be reduced. Usually, the budget trimming will happen in the stages of your app's production before the engineering process begins. Chris Pautsch, CEO of KeylimeTie, tells clients to keep their budget to themselves at first. "We do not want to hear the budget upfront. We are giving a true-to-form cost and effort of what we think it is going to take," explained Chris. Most developers will ask for a budget before they begin scoping a project, take Chris's advice and keep it private to prevent any biased or misleading pricing.

Both freelancers and design studios have their strengths and weaknesses.

GEOGRAPHIC

If possible, try to find a developer that allows you to meet face-to-face. You want the ability to have meetings, talk in person, and establish a relationship with the people building your app. Professionals who care about their clients will also strive to build a mutual working relationship.

In the instances where that is not possible, make sure video calls or conferencing will be allowed. Whether that be through FaceTime or Skype, video calls are a must. Phone calls, e-mails, and text messages will not suffice for your project.
Communication with your developer is important. Almost every individual I interviewed mentioned the necessity of easy and open communication.

FREELANCERS

A freelancer will work for an hourly wage; most likely, a freelancer would work independently of any company or hierarchy. Most freelancers are professional developers. Freelancers can even be undergraduate computer-science majors looking to get their feet wet. Many projects use freelancers located in foreign countries such as India.

OFFSHORING

Offshoring is a tricky topic, and each scenario should be taken on a case-by-case basis. Design studios and freelancers can both be located offshore. Often, international development firms will have a business development office in the United States. Business development is a fancy term for sales. A domestic sales team does not guarantee quality. Regardless of where the business development office is located, you need to be more diligent in your research than you would be for a domestic developer. If you decide to offshore, design studios are a safer choice than freelancers.

Besides asking about their design and development process, find out what country they are located, how they accept payment, and pertinent contact information. The world is not always in equilibrium, and regional instability can affect your app's development. Second, you do not want to be doing business with a country where rampant fraud and tech crimes are committed. Hence, how they accept payment is important. You do not want to wire transfer your payment overseas or reveal any other information that could be easily compromised. Finally, contact information is needed to assess prior projects, read reviews, and determine who your main point of contact will be. During my research, I encountered sentiment across the spectrum regarding offshoring. Most of that sentiment was unfavorable, yet most conceded it was possible under the right circumstances.

TIME

Your time frame can be both a positive and a negative when considering offshoring. "If time is not important then offshoring makes a lot of sense," said John Ostler, cofounder of Eight Bit Studios. "If time is not important, you can fail a couple times and might not run out of funds and still do something about it." Offshoring firms or freelancers may be slow to produce deliverables. If there is an urgent need for your product, an offshore developer may not be the best decision. A slow production process could lose momentum, and your initial burning passion for the project may simmer.

On the other hand, your app idea may be a long-term project rather than one that requires immediate attention. You will be able to cheaply iterate your app several times over a longer period. "If time is no object, then offshoring is worth the risk. If you are urgent and serious about solving a problem, offshoring does not make sense."

Besides your time frame, think of the time zone your offshore developer is located in. App development should be an inclusive process between both the client and the developer. It will be hard to coordinate and communicate effectively if you are in the United States and your developer is in Bangladesh. You will be sleeping as they are working—not exactly an ideal scenario. If you need to offshore, try to find developers that are north or south of you. Finding people located in countries north or south of you will at least decrease or offset the impact of time zones.

LANGUAGE BARRIER

Being crystal clear, defining your objectives, and having open communications with everybody involved in your process has been hammered throughout this book. It can be challenging to achieve those three items with a language barrier. Intricate and detailed features might be hard to explain if the people creating your app do not understand you. You also cannot be generic in your instructions to developers. It is a beatable hurdle but nevertheless still an additional challenge that you will not face with a domestic developer. If you choose an offshore developer, make sure your foreign developer speaks and writes in proficient English.

OFFSHORING COSTS

Yes, upfront costs such as hourly development wages are usually cheaper offshore, but your app's quality may reflect it. Second, an offshore design firm may have redundant costs. One example, you might need two project managers to coordinate between the different locations and teams. Do not get too excited when you see an offshore design studio with surprisingly low upfront prices. It may be misleading. "If you want a quick-and-dirty prototype, you can absolutely offshore," said Greg Raiz, CEO of Raizlabs. "If you want to build a large business off it, I would not recommend it." Sometimes, startups will start their project offshore and transition their development to a domestic firm. Don't just go scraping the bottom of the barrel hoping to find a cheap developer. "You can definitely find inexpensive development, but it is hard to find the level of quality you'll need to be successful," explained Greg.

OFFSHORING HORROR STORIES

As the founder of Ethervision, Randall Cross has encountered his fair share of outsourcing horror stories. Ethervision was one of the first mobile app development studios for iOS and Android in the Midwest United States, possibly the very first one. Randall specializes in enterprise mobile development and business strategy and execution. Ethervision will sometimes be recruited to patch up a hack job by an overseas developer. I always ask design studios their objective opinion about outsourcing development; Randall did not mince words. "A guy off the street looking to build an app does not know the right questions," said Randall. Without a firm understanding of technical lingo and experience with apps, it can be easy to be taken advantage of. He maintains there are still a lot of "shady folks" involved with outsourcing.

"They will keep [your project] going for a while, send you test builds, and fake functionality. Suddenly, you're on a conference call and they cannot understand you," explained Randall. "After understanding you for weeks, these developers might begin to claim the language barrier is a problem." By doing this, developers can remove themselves from a half-assed project and take their earnings with them.

Randall states the recourse of action is very small. He joked, "The only option you have is to go shake them down yourself." I do not believe Randall is pessimistic about outsourcing as an industry, but he is cognizant the opportunity is rife for a naïve entrepreneur to get ripped off. Do not engage with international developers without doing extensive research.

Ethervision is not the only developer telling entrepreneurs to tread carefully. Greg Raiz, CEO and founder of Raizlabs, mentioned his firm has rescued numerous projects that were butchered by offshore developers. Developers at Hashrocket also salvaged a project after the client's offshore developers went offline because of political turmoil in Eastern Europe.

NO PING PONG TABLES

Shervin Delband has lived and worked in California his whole life. Shervin was once employed as a software engineer for Burstly, a company acquired by Apple in 2014. His early exposure to offshoring validated his negative opinions. "They played games like holding the code hostage, developers were never accessible, and they kept their engineering teams behind the curtains," stated Shervin. "When I worked as an Android developer, I would never start a project from scratch, but takeover damaged projects started offshore." He mentioned the offshore firms he encountered had a habit of overpromising and underdelivering.

Today, Shervin is a partner and the director of U.S. operations at ITRex Group, a firm that does all their development work offshore. ITRex Group is perhaps most famous for building the Dollar Shave Club app. Shervin's dramatic change of heart towards offshoring happened after being impressed by the work ethic of a Belarus firm. Belarus is an Eastern European country, formerly part of the Soviet Union. After the Belarus firm helped Shervin with a project, Shervin believed he could help the offshore firm earn business. Together, they formed the ITRex Group.

In their first year, ITRex Group earned over $1 million in revenue. It was not always easy though. Shervin had a hard time convincing clients his offshore team was different. To ensure quality, he hires good developers with a firm understanding of the fundamentals. Today, there are over sixty engineers that are overseen by a management team that has accountability. "It all starts with quality," explained Shervin. "Earning domestic business is hard enough with the stigma that surrounds offshoring. If we do not deliver quality, there is no word of mouth business." After speaking with Shervin, it was clear he understood how to overcome offshoring's negative stigma. Before hiring an offshore developer, there are several things to consider.

First, make sure the offshore team does not relax their hiring standards. Often, teams will hire more people to manage the workflow thus sacrificing quality. Inquire about the fundamentals and experience needed to become a software engineer at their overseas development office.

Second, the engineers should have ownership over their work and check their code daily. "You want engineers that put their feet down," said Shervin. "I want my engineers to take longer and do it the right way, not just take the quick-and-dirty path to completion." Shervin believes some countries produce better software engineers. All engineers working for ITRex are from Belarus or Ukraine. "There is a strong sense of order and duty in the Eastern European culture. There are no complaints or excuses and this translates to their work. When the engineers are really good you do not need all the extra stuff like playing ping pong throughout the day." By playing ping pong, Shervin is referring to the laidback culture of many design and software engineering firms in the United States. "Overseas give them the task and a screenshot of what it should look like and they just get it done." Also, make sure that their work is being tested by somebody in the United States.

Third, being extra proactive with communication and feedback can make remote situations work. Provide enough information so the offshore team can stay busy without making any assumptions. As I mentioned before, some offshore teams are located on the opposite side of the world and are working while you are sleeping. Providing them with enough detail allows them to get their task completed. The overseas engineers' ability to communicate is also important. Overcoming the language barrier is a must. At ITRex Group, Shervin wants all his software engineers to at least be proficient in written English.

Offshoring is usually an attractive option because of cheaper development costs. Shervin clarified that hiring an offshore developer can be cheaper than hiring domestically. A lot of startups with little capital will begin their project offshore and transition their work to a domestic firm. Shervin will usually help interview domestic firms to ensure quality is matched once the project comes home.

It only takes one bad experience with an offshore team to make somebody permanently opposed to the practice so Shervin works hard to curate and maintain ITRex Group's quality.

DESIGN STUDIOS

Design studios employ multiple engineers, designers, programmers, and other digital artisans that develop technologies. Other names for a design studio include design agency, consultancy, or firm. You may find this book biased toward design studios, specifically domestic firms, and that is intentional. A design studio will undoubtedly be more expensive than a freelancer, but the long-term benefits may outweigh the initial costs. A single freelancer cannot possibly be skilled in all aspects of app development. The culmination and collaboration of creative and technical talent in a design studio cannot be matched by a single freelancer. If there are freelancers who can do everything your app requires, their fees are probably comparable to a full-suite design team.

You can find a design studio using the website clutch.co. It gives visitors a quick glance that breaks down a studio's portfolio, price range, and reviews in easy-to-read modules. Undoubtedly, there are other good websites to find a design studio, but this is an industry favorite.

PARTNERS OR INVESTORS

No, the design studio does not want to help fund your project. Design studios need to pay their bills like any other company. They cannot afford to fund or partially fund the cost of your project. Often, entrepreneurs or startups get the wrong idea that design studios build the best ideas. Wrong. Design studios build funded projects that align with their interests or mission.

Rarely will a developer work for free, including freelancers. An independent third party in the business of making apps is not the best choice for a technical cofounder. If you want to be taken seriously by a developer, do not mention partnering or cofounding during initial conversations. Asking a studio to partner or cofound the app with you is an immediate signal that you do not have funding or you want a discount on the price. Often, aspiring entrepreneurs will want a cofounder with development skills to save costs on development and design in exchange for ownership equity. Design studios are not a ripe opportunity for such a scenario. You are more likely to find a cofounder among a freelancing crowd, specifically one you already know and trust.

Too many ideas and app projects walk through a developer's doors; it would be impossible for studios to vouch for each one. However, they can become instrumental in providing prototypes and other materials used in a pitch.

Design studios occasionally accept a partnership or cofound an app, but usually this is initiated by the studio. If the offer comes, consider the proposal. Until then, do not mention it.

HONESTY AND OPEN COMMUNICATIONS

Design studios will talk to dozens of people per day about their ideas. They are constantly coordinating between multiple individuals attempting to determine the scope of a submitted idea. Sales, project managers, and developers must contribute to the scope. It can be an enormous undertaking. Do not waste their time.

Be upfront about where you are in the process. If you have no funding, tell them. If you have funding but no company or strategy…tell them. Relay the amount of experience you have with apps. Your person of contact in the design studio has most likely dealt with hundreds of individuals in the same situation as you. They understand the complexities and challenges of building an app and will not judge you or your progress. You will find that most studios are willing to provide free feedback and advice.

Your long-term relationship with any design studio will benefit from honesty about your intentions. Being crystal clear is most important when coordinating with the people responsible for building your app. You should also receive the same openness and honesty from your developer or studio. Anything less than clear, truthful communication between both parties is grounds for termination of the relationship.

FAMOUS CLIENTS

Many design studios display their portfolio of work and clientele on their websites. It can be easy for the logos of famous brands in their portfolio to sway opinion or earn business. Bob Hagenberg, director of business development at Robosoft Technologies, warns entrepreneurs of getting sucked up into the hype stemming from a misleading client portfolio. "Everybody works with companies like Walmart, Disney, or ESPN because they have outsourcing programs," said Bob. "Be careful. It does not necessarily mean [these developers] built an app from ground zero all the way to the end." Before getting excited, Bob cautions entrepreneurs to ask the studio about the extent of their work with large companies. Public or global companies often have their own development and design segments. Often, these departments become overwhelmed, and the company decides to alleviate the work load through a third party. In most cases, these design studios only work within a small facet of their clients' web or mobile application products.

I'll use Groupon as an example because several of the studios I talked to listed Groupon as a client. Because a design studio lists Groupon as a client does not necessarily mean they developed and designed Groupon from scratch. They may have helped with a software patch, a specific application, or another smaller project that contributes to Groupon's overall digital presence.

If the famous brands on their website marquee impress you, be sure to inquire the extent of their work with those clients. The inclusion of global or well-known brands is meant to bolster reputations and earn new business. Do not get sucked into the hype.

MORE THAN REVENUE

You want a studio that is both competent and honest. Your business should mean more to them than their bottom line. Most studios will accept a project because it aligns with their values or mission. Raizlabs, based in Boston and Oakland, only builds apps that improve lives through technology. Their founder, Greg Raiz, told me they want clients who are looking to make a positive impact on humanity. Other companies such as Table XI focus on small- to medium-sized businesses and happily work with mission-driven businesses. Whatever your app or idea might be, seek the right studio for the job. An alignment of values and personalities will give both parties an appropriate footing moving forward.

Aside from an alignment on values, logistics also need to be considered. The level of client engagement required by the developer varies so it's important you have this discussion beforehand. "Ensure everyone is aligned. This should include a discussion around how available the client will need to be, when weekly status and other meetings should take place, when feedback is expected from the clients, turnaround time for client to-do lists, the approval process, and risk management," stated Heather Brown, director of project management at Eight Bit Studios. Follow Heather's advice and inquire about the level of commitment expected from you.

REAL PROJECTS

Some people get an idea on a Saturday night and are emailing developers by Monday morning about their idea. Experienced design studios will immediately recognize this type of behavior. "One of the first indicators of an entrepreneur's seriousness is how much work they have already done before approaching us," said Brett Mackie of Eight Bit Studios. As the director of accounts and managing partner, Brett is responsible for having an internal and visceral understanding of what it takes to introduce a minimum viable product. Since 2008, Brett has been exposed to clients in all stages of development. "We are interested in the type of research already done, and if they have validated their idea with the public. We also ask if these individuals have spoken to their friends or family about their app or built any sort of prototype." Eight Bit Studios wants competitive research to be completed before acceptance of a project. Regularly, aspiring entrepreneurs will have an idea for an app that already exists. If an app already exists, that does not mean you are out of the game. Make sure your idea is an improvement or a provides a better solution than existing apps.

Brett says his studio is "incredibly stoked when somebody walks in with a prototype. There are varying ways on what a prototype might do, but if you have had the ability to test and validate that main feature, it makes our job much easier." A lack of research will be a red flag for busy design studios that cannot afford to entertain every idea that is floated their way. Have a firm understanding of your idea and you will enter conversations with developers from a position of strength.

REJECTED

Just because you have an idea, it does not guarantee a developer will work with you or that the app will get made. Even with your project funded, studios might reject your project or refuse to prepare a proposal for you. I spoke to several design studios about their clients and projects. There are a variety of reasons a design studio may refuse your project. Please note that these are just some examples from several studios.

Although design studios are normally for-profit, your business may not always be welcome. Several studios told me that an entrepreneur who has liquidated their life savings to self-finance their project will be rejected. Responsible and trustworthy studios want to know where your capital comes from because they are not in the business of taking somebody's last dollar. Bootstrapping is important, but self-financing can be too extreme depending on an individual's net worth or financial situation. Multiple studios also mentioned they will reject an app project if all its capital is allocated toward development, leaving nothing for advertising or marketing.

Studios may also reject you for unrealistic expectations. "If the general interest is to just quickly sell something, it tells us there is only short term interest and not something we would like to be involved with. We don't like the 'get-rich' projects," said Brett Mackie, director of accounts at Eight Bit Studios. As mentioned earlier in the book, seeking an acquisition is challenging and not a viable strategy.

Another question asked by every studio: can we work with this team? Team dynamics is essential to all developers. Most studios like their clients to be hands-on, which requires a lot of interaction and communication. Danny Saad, vice president of engineering at Dom & Tom, said they have met a lot of dangerous personalities over the years. "We need to really work as partners with our clients and build something compelling. Sometimes personalities are not compatible."

Saad also mentioned a product idea may not be viable. Dom & Tom has found that some ideas may be too risky at the current time because the technology does not currently exist. Dom & Tom, as do all other studios, want to be able to guarantee deliverables needed by the client.

Remarkably, every studio I spoke to mentioned they will always recommend other studios if they reject a project.

RETAINER FEES

Be cautious with individuals or studios that charge retainer fees. A retainer fee is an upfront cost to ensure services are rendered. The studio that created the first version of Bistro Bash felt a little large for my project. At the time, this studio was well known and a rising star. Hence, the retainer fee seemed like a reasonable price at the time. I was writing an enormous check at the first of the month to pay their heavy retainer fee. Since I was paying a retainer, the clock was always ticking until the next month began. All decisions had to be made quickly, and time cannot be paused.

The first few weeks are essential to getting your app right, and at the very least, you should have control over the pace of the project. I'll give you an example. It was the second week of production, and designs for the Bistro Bash logo were starting to trickle in. I was not very happy with any of them because they seemed to be missing my vision. However, I could not waste any time with deciding because of the inflexible timetable laid out with the retainer. Each week a certain milestone had to be reached. Otherwise, the scope would have expanded beyond my budget. I ended up choosing a logo I was somewhat happy with instead of one that I was jubilant about.

However, retainer fees will not be the bane of your app's existence. Throughout my research, I came across several studios that charged a retainer fee but delivered an agreed-upon first version, aka minimum viable product (MVP). Before taking their client's money, the client and the studio would decide what needed to be included in an MVP and sign an agreement to deliver it for a flat fee. In this scenario, a retainer might appear both reasonable and viable. Otherwise, do not pay a retainer fee until your deliverables are guaranteed in plain writing regardless of the timetable. Sometimes, a developer may entice potential clients by promising an unrealistic number of features, but once payment has exchanged hands, the scope shrinks, desired features are chopped up, and a weaker product will be the result.

COMMITMENT

Conventional wisdom tells us that we are not supposed to buy the first car we test drive. The same advice should be applied to shopping for a developer. Reach out to domestic freelancers, offshore design studios, domestic design studios, and everything in between. Get as many price points as possible. When these developers scope your project, they should detail the cost and time needed to make every proposed featured. This will allow you to compare prices and shop around.

Usually these scopes and prices will be presented in a proposal. Not only will the proposal lay out features with their associated cost, but deliverables will be mentioned. A deliverable is something that is going to be provided by your developer. Second, design studios will usually guarantee their top-notch talent for every project, and generally they deliver on that promise. However, there are instances where the top-notch talent is removed from your app after development commences. Make sure these studios abide by their promises and put it in writing.

Third, you must be able to trust your developer. An untrustworthy developer can sabotage your app or mess with your developer licenses. With no technical experience, you will be none the wiser and have no way to prove a developer intentionally sabotaged your programming. If a dispute arises, you should have good faith your developer will act professionally and maintain its integrity.

Finally, do not choose a developer because it is the cheapest option. Aside from cost, find a developer you will be able to work with for the foreseeable future and maintain a healthy relationship with. Do not count on your app becoming self-sufficient to the point you can hire your own internal development team. The people building your app should be the people you want to get in the trenches with. As you have discovered, your app is going to face considerable headwinds, and you want a developer that will fully support you when the going gets tough.

How to Succeed:

- Don't reveal your budget before your app is scoped.
- Try to find a developer that you can easily communicate with.
- Your time frame is important when considering developers.
- Most design studios do not want to lower their prices in exchange for equity in your project.
- Offshoring can be a considerable risk.

- Be honest with your developer about your intentions and goals.
- Find a developer that aligns with your personal values. Finding the cheapest developer is not always the best move.
- Developers that charge a retainer fee may not be the best choice to build your app's first version.
- Talk with multiple developers of different backgrounds before committing to one.

7

PROTECTING YOURSELF & FUNDING

Regardless of your technical expertise you are going to need funds to build, release, and support your app. Most likely, you will need the app built by a third party. In the event a third party is building your app, the scope of your project should determine the amount of capital needed. As you now know, app developers rarely work for free, and initial development will not be the sole cost of your app.

Additionally, you will need adequate funds to cover other expenses such as the following items:

- Advertising and marketing
- Feature upgrades
- Ongoing maintenance
- Legal
- Compensation

I cannot possibly infer the socioeconomic status, wealth, or connections of my readers. As a result, this chapter mainly discusses what to look for and consider when raising capital rather than where to look.

SKIN IN THE GAME

Most individuals pitch an idea or concept to venture capitalists, but Kyle Henry pitched a business plan. He maintains the business plan itself was garbage, but it grabbed the attention of the venture capitalist. After leaving Wall Street in 2010, Kyle vowed to use his abilities in finance, strategy, and data analysis toward social and environmental initiatives.

Kyle was hired for his financial skill set and became the entrepreneur in residence. His new employer was making an exorbitant amount of money from a single company and needed new ventures to invest the capital overflow. While Kyle was the entrepreneur in residence, he created financial projections for several companies that altogether received an $11 million investment. His venture capitalist career was off to a good start. Since joining the startup community, Kyle's teams have successfully raised $17 million in early-stage investments. He has experience in multiple industries including recycled packaging, hydroponic agriculture, local-farm food distribution, mobile e-commerce apps, and productivity software tools among others.

Today, Kyle Henry is the cofounder and managing director of Venturesome, the first company to bring proven entrepreneurs into corporations and foundations to execute strategic innovation initiatives.

I asked Kyle what are the key points he looks for in a pitch. Not surprisingly, he wants entrepreneurs to have "skin in the game, either time or money already invested." Kyle and I both agree that without skin in the game, an individual can bounce at the first sign of trouble. However, too much investment by the founder can become problematic. A sentiment also echoed by design studios I spoke too. "Sometimes it is sad if people put too much of their own money in. There is a healthy amount of skin in the game. It allows the founder to balance smart decisions and show dedication," explained Kyle. Venture capitalists do not want somebody whose sole motivation is to save what remains of their liquidated 401(k) or life savings.

For the most part, raising capital will be nearly impossible without your time or money being invested in some capacity. Skin in the game, as it is commonly referred to, will keep you focused and motivated.

BUILD YOUR STRATEGY

Kyle Henry was once the chief marketing officer for Tide Spin. Tide Spin is an app-based laundry service that offers free delivery and no minimum order amount. Unlike most apps, Tide

Spin is powered by an all-American brand, Tide, and its parent company, Procter & Gamble. Recently, large multinational corporations have ventured into the startup space to spur innovation.

Tide Spin was the new player in the growing on-demand laundry services market, and Kyle needed to speak to the experts. At the time, the now-defunct Washio ruled the on-demand laundry service racket.

Kyle recognized that Tide Spin was an amalgamation of three functions: technology, logistics, and cleaning. Procter & Gamble and Tide, naturally, were cleaning experts so he skipped seeking advice in this area. Kyle focused his time researching and speaking with on-demand delivery startups, dry cleaning store owners, and software companies that worked with residential buildings in Chicago. The insights and understanding of the business ecosystem drove the strategy and rapid prototyping process that his team executed over the next few months.

"Expertise is everything," said Kyle. "The first stage should not be limited to customer or market research, so you talk to the experts." The insight provided by logistics companies allowed Tide Spin to cut delivery costs and build a long-term strategy. Additionally, Kyle agrees most experts are typically interested in sharing their knowledge.

It is relatively easy to find an expert willing to talk with you. On the other hand, I am not advocating you to e-mail Stephen Hawking and ask him to explain general relativity and quantum mechanics for your cosmology app. To find primary sources for this book, I would simply use the "Contact Us" form on many websites. Be crystal clear with your intentions, contact as many people as possible through these "Contact" forms, and wait to see who responds. Search for companies or universities in your area—somebody will be willing to discuss their experience or expertise with you.

Besides finding experts on your concept, look for successful entrepreneurs with prior app experience. Cyrus Kiani, founder of TouchZen Media and project manager at CitrusBits, would agree with Kyle. Cyrus understands the importance of seeking expert advice; he even flew from the United States to Stockholm, Sweden to meet an entrepreneur he admired. "Find somebody that has made a successful app or an app that you love," said Cyrus. He advises aspiring entrepreneurs to write down a list of every app they love, contact the developers, and see who responds. Their experience may not only be relatable but also save you from making costly mistakes such as choosing the wrong developer or focusing on the wrong features. Converging the information from both experts on your concept and apps like your own proposed app will help you put together a solid business plan.

Kyle said a business plan should be a good framework. The best business plans "start with the end in mind" and detail the expertise, capabilities, and capital needed to achieve a company's near term goals. Although these plans will not be able to predict the future nor be perfect, it at least allows an investor to examine an entrepreneur's thought process and a concept's viability.

For Bistro Bash, I lacked a coherent strategy and business plan. The result and fate of Bistro Bash should be used as an example of their importance. If an app is a business, it is imperative for a business plan to exist.

SIX-SECONDS OF FAME

In 2013, Vine became a millennial social-networking craze that challenged popular conventions. The popular app allowed users to upload only six-second looped videos and the time constraint bred unmatched creativity. It was once the most downloaded free app in the iOS App Store. By 2014, it had more than 40 million users. Obscure no-names became celebrities after garnering thousands and sometimes millions of followers from quirky, creative videos. Brittany Furlan, spent ten years in Hollywood chasing fame but became an overnight celebrity on Vine. Similarly, a teenager from North Carolina named Nash Grier became the most famous Vine celebrity in the world after amassing more than 12.7 million Vine followers addicted to his comedic content. Usually, these Vine celebrities would expand their brand into larger sites such as YouTube, Facebook, Instagram, and Snapchat. At one point, Furlan was earning between $7,000 and $20,000 per six-second clip. Over a hundred million people per month were watching Vine videos. Burberry, General Electric, Coca-Cola, and other household name brands were rushing to establish a presence on the social media platform. Today, Vine is all but gone.

In 2017, Twitter, Vine's parent company, shuttered the Vine social network. Now, all that remains is an app called Vine Camera that allows people to shoot six-second videos and upload them to Twitter. Vine was acquired by Twitter in 2012 for a reported $30 million. Vine's potential return on investment was always questioned. Like Twitter itself, Vine had an ambiguous vision. The company never shared in the fortunes of its beloved creators and failed to catch up with the other social media juggernauts. Brands were paying the popular Vine stars directly to mention or showcase their products. Vine had missed a tremendous early opportunity to become a middle man for these transactions. In an attempt to capitalize on lost ground, Twitter purchased Niche, an agency that works with social media creators and brands to create meaningful content.

After refusing to accept the demands of their newly minted celebrities, the most popular Vine stars collectively walked away from the platform in 2016. Shortly after their departure, Twitter announced in October that Vine would eventually be shuttered. Vine is hardly an anomaly. Even Twitter has struggled to impress investors as it faces identity issues and slowing growth. In their 2016 annual report, Twitter describes itself as "a global platform for public self-expression and conversation in real-time." However, they think of themselves as a broadcasting, social media, and news company. These are three facets that do not always naturally coexist. Users are concerned about privacy, safety, spam, and hostility from other people on the platform. Internet trolls and terrorist propaganda have been hot topics the social media giant has yet to fully tackle. However, Twitter is a successful public company that earned over $2.5 billion in revenue during 2016, so they can afford a somewhat incoherent vision. A new startup built around a single app cannot afford to build a product first and think about a strategy later.

WAYS TO MAKE MONEY

There are several ways to make money with an app. Never assume a certain model is best for your app. Once you validate people will use your product, figure out when and where people will spend money to access your app and its content. These revenue models are not rigid. In fact, you will find many successful apps incorporate several of these models simultaneously. These are some of your options:

Paid Apps

A paid app will charge users a fee to download the app.

In-App Purchases

Power-ups. Unlockable or additional content. Extra features. Emojis. In-app purchases are found in almost every app. For example, Facebook Messenger charges users a fee if they want to buy additional stickers. Pokémon Go offers in-game content such as Lure Models or Lucky Eggs, which gamers can purchase. Candy Crush Saga is notable for having tremendous success with in-app purchases. Users purchased more than $1.3 billion of in-app content in 2014 alone; however, do not assume people will want to spend money in your app just because content is available for purchase. Figure out what users want and what they will actually purchase. Many apps with in-app purchases have no upfront fee. These are referred to as "freemium" apps.

Ad-Based Model, or Free Apps

There are still a lot of free apps in the app markets. Having a free app does not mean there is no business model. If, and that is a big *if*, you can get enough eyeballs looking and interacting with your app, advertisements can be displayed in your app. A business plan with an ad-based model is risky. It is almost like using "hope" as a strategy.

Subscriptions

Subscriptions are becoming increasingly popular across all technology services, including apps. According to the App Store website, "users can buy in-app purchases to access content, services, and experiences for renewable or non-renewing durations." Almost all subscription services offer auto-renew options and are relatively inexpensive. Popular services that use subscription models include Apple Music, Spotify, Tinder, and Amazon Prime. Subscriptions encourage repeat users and can help maintain a growth in active users. By providing new content, your app is less likely to be abandoned. Most apps using the freemium model or advertisements see peaks and valleys in engagement and revenue. Subscription models can help create stability.

Commission

Your app does not necessarily need to make money from consumers. The gig economy operates on commissions and small fees. On-demand or gig economy apps earn revenue through commissions on services provided through the app. Many apps that are business-to-business rely on commission or fees in exchange for their provided services.

Although these are all viable sources of revenue, subscription-based models are becoming more commonplace and encouraged. "The main advantage is it provides for a steady revenue stream, and this generally aligns with developers providing continued value to their customers," explained Greg Raiz, CEO of Raizlabs. "Apps that have a one-time revenue stream have a difficulty growing because the lifetime value of the customer is low. With a subscription model, there is continued interest in adding features to the app." However, creating an app that encourages ongoing usage and engagement is a hefty challenge. "The downside is that customers may be unwilling to pay for a subscription model if they don't feel they are getting continuous improvements."

Ultimately, the type of app you make will dictate how you earn revenue. If you are working with an experienced developer, he or she will probably nudge you one way or another. However, try to establish how you will make money as you put your app together. As you gauge an audience interest during conversation, it is necessary to know not only whether they will use the app, but if they will pay for it.

For more information on business models, go to the Apple Developer website and find the page titled "Choosing a Business Model."

FINDING INVESTORS

The most difficult part of this entire process will be finding investors. My first recommendation when raising capital would be to stay away from individuals in your close inner circle or family. In any business, there will always be complications or disagreements, and it is best to keep those at arm's length. Relationships should never be put in jeopardy because of a business or vice versa. At some point, investors will disagree with the moves you make, and you do not want friction with people you see often.

EXPECT TO LOSE MONEY

Make sure your investors know that creating an app is like the Hail Mary pass I discussed in chapter 2. They are going to be putting their chips on the table with the strong possibility of never seeing those chips again; however, the prospect of an extreme return will keep them interested in the investment. Investing in an app is exciting, and not many people get the chance to do so.

Generally, people who often do not have the opportunity to invest in projects like this will be your first investors. It is a lot more exciting than investing in the stock market.

A fantastic product and excellent business plan will not necessarily change the odds in your favor. During the first quarter of 2016, the top 1 percent of paid apps or free apps with in-app purchases accounted for 94 percent of the US App Store's revenue. SensorTower estimated $1.34 billion of the projected $1.43 billion in sales went to only 623 publishers. The remaining $86 million was spread among nearly 67,000 publishers. Most of those 67,000 publishers probably did not earn enough to pay their bills.

Concerns about app profitability for the average developer has been a continuous trend among all app markets. It will always be hard to estimate future revenue or cash flows of your app. As a result, investing in an unproven app developed by an inexperienced entrepreneur will never be the safest investment. Make sure your investors know this before you both sign the dotted line.

MORE THAN MONEY

Most importantly, you should find investors who bring some unique skill or connection related to your app. I think my biggest mistake was only having two investors who truly had tangible resources that could relate to Bistro Bash. I often wonder how different things would have been if I had at my disposal a team of investors who understood the restaurant industry, mobile games, and the media. Because they are investors, they are automatically vested in the success of the app. More likely than not, their expertise or time will be inexpensive and beneficial.

UNDERSTANDING THE APP MARKET

Finally, you need investors who use or understand mobile apps. My investors were terrific; they took a chance with me and, for the most part, were patient. Individuals who have always worked in a tangible world might not understand the problems of a digital one. Although apps are a business, they do not function like typical businesses of the past. Additionally, downloads and revenue are not directly correlated. Therefore, expectations are all over the table. This is what some individuals might have an issue with grasping. Just because you have x number of downloads does not guarantee y in revenue. For example, a million downloads does not guarantee an equal return from each user. You may have several hundred-people using your app on a daily basis, but there is a chance not a single in-app purchase will be made by any users.

There is no secret formula to predict how well your app will turn downloads or active users into revenue. These metrics will not be discovered until your app has been released to the public and you can quantify a user's engagement with your platform. I wish I understood this before I made Bistro Bash. It would not have stopped me from making Bistro Bash, but I would have clarified that to potential investors immediately.

JUDGMENT

It is best to use your own judgment in all scenarios and make compromises where they are needed. You may be fortunate enough that you only need one investor. Although unlikely, an angel investor might bless you with a blank check to get the app built. If that happens, first some congratulations are in order. Not many people get an angel investor to cover their entire project before it even starts. Second, try to find other investors. Do not deny their money, but tell them you would first like to find other investors who can bring something more to the app than just their checkbook before closing off your first round of funding.

SET UP A BANK ACCOUNT

This should be a no-brainer: go to a bank and open a business bank account. Keep your personal finances separate. Not to mention, you are dealing with the digital realm, and you will need a form of electronic banking. Keeping several hundred grand under your mattress won't cut it. You will need an Employer Identification Number (EIN) to open a business bank account, so make sure you have your legal entity established before going to the bank.

STEAL YOUR IDEA

Talking to other aspiring entrepreneurs or app dreamers, I often noticed people were concerned somebody would steal their idea, run away with it, and make millions. I attribute this to *The Social Network*, the popular Hollywood film depicting the proliferation of Facebook starring Jesse Eisenberg as Mark Zuckerberg. Although you should be aware of these potential conflicts, do not sweat them too much. Chris Pautsch, the founder of KeyLimeTie laughed off this issue. Chris said there are always individuals claiming to "have an idea that is going to revolutionize the world" and they are excessively protective of their app. Often, potential clients will immediately discuss non-disclosure agreements, also known as NDAs, and patents. For most developers, this is an easy indication of inexperience. If all you have is an app idea, getting a patent should be the least of your concerns. A patent will be a waste of time and resources. Instead of worrying about somebody stealing your idea, focus on executing the idea and making it successful. You are not building a flying car or brewing a formula to cure cancer. An app idea does not warrant an immediate need for patents. Most developers will give you full rights to all materials related to your app once your debts to them are paid, but make sure this is established in writing before signing any contracts with a developer.

Nate Schier, a partner at Sidebench, said, "Ideas are worth nothing. Half the people we talk to they want to sign an NDA right away. They are showing that they are not really mature or don't know how this works. We are not going to steal their idea. An idea is worth nothing to us."

As you have discovered, building and releasing an app is not an easy process, nor is development cheap. Studios and developers get paid to build apps, they are not going to waste their time stealing your idea. A studio that likes your idea enough to build it for free will expect you to be part of the process. Are there shady developers out there? Yes, but professional developers, especially design studios, try to maintain honorable reputations to earn big business. If you are that concerned somebody is going to steal your idea, have them sign an NDA, but be nonchalant about it. An NDA will not prevent your idea from being stolen; however, it gives you credibly and creates a subtle aura of legitimacy. The NDA will allow you to have substantive evidence that your idea is your personal intellectual property. Be professional when mandating an NDA should be signed and be selective who you share your ideas with. Stay away from using phrases like "my app will start a revolution" or "change the world" or "make a billion dollars."

FINDING A GOOD LAWYER

If you are reading this book, it is probably your first time attempting to build an app. It is going to be exciting, nerve-racking, and wonderful. Keep in mind, though, that you are bound to make mistakes. These will become fantastic learning experiences although they might not seem like that at the time. Simple mistakes can create long-term, complex problems. These mistakes are easy to identify in retrospect and will be valuable to you in the future.

One of the earliest mistakes I made was in my search for an NDA. I was hooked up with a lawyer through a friend, and I was young and naïve. The lawyer took me through the ringer, charging me several hundred dollars for what appeared to be a basic NDA with my company name inserted throughout. I should have immediately known this lawyer was shady. He was almost an hour late to our first and only meeting. His office did not even have a name on the door and he was the only employee. If a situation does not feel right, do not be afraid to walk away.

When searching for attorneys, try to find somebody who is not only cheap, but also somebody you can trust. My next attorney was set-up through family members and had experience with setting up high-risk entities. I did not have that problem again.

Before Bistro Bash was launched, my former employer offered to take on the legal work for my company. This former employer and friend became my new lawyer. He was a terrific helping hand and became an investor himself. Not everybody will be as fortunate as I was in this scenario, but if you seek out the right people the chips should fall into place.

An attorney becomes a necessity when you decide to raise capital. Investors will not just hand you bags of cash hoping you abide by the honor system when it comes to their equity stake. Before you raise capital, build your advisory board. An advisory board populated with business professionals can serve you well in the long run and prevent you from making novice mistakes. Besides helping you find an attorney and establish a legal entity, an advisory board comprised of business professionals will help with basic bookkeeping practices.

MANAGING EXPENSES

During your app's lifecycle, you will be hard-pressed to spend like crazy to promote your app, hire people, or upgrade features. Instead of directly spending your cash, try to maximize your efforts and current resources. Although large corporations and established companies have abundant resources, you have the freedom to be creative with no rules or red tape holding you back. Before you spend your cash, ask yourself if you can do the task yourself. As a first-time entrepreneur, it was always tempting to outsource work and spend money on menial or small tasks. At one point, I had $100,000 in cash sitting in the bank. Generating small expenses was not difficult. However, small expenses eventually add up to sizable outflows. Exercise discipline and show restraint when deciding how and when to spend cash.

How to Succeed:

- Nobody will steal your app idea so do not rush to find a lawyer and waste money on an NDA.
- No, patents are not necessary.
- Having your own "skin in the game" is important.
- Find investors that understand the risks of investing in apps.
- Investors should bring more to the table besides just their checkbook.
- Inquire through conversation whether people will pay money to use your app.
- Find a trustworthy lawyer to set up an entity that allows you to raise sufficient capital. Remember, your app's capital needs extend beyond just the initial costs of development.
- Create a strategy that shows investors how you will achieve your objectives and pay them back.
- Populate your advisory board with business professionals.

8

PRODUCTION

Production will be a different experience for you. Your ideas are no longer under your control, and your contribution may be limited.

Before the app goes into production, you are going to notice some changes from the original idea. In fact, you may find yourself repeating or optimizing many of the strategies laid forth in chapter 3.

CREATE A DEVELOPER ACCOUNT

Every app market requires a developer account to publish apps. If your developer has any experience with apps, he or she should be able to assist you with establishing an account. Navigating these accounts can be tricky with no prior experience as they are not user-friendly to those with no technical education.

UP-TO-DATE

If Bistro Bash had been built immediately upon the idea's conception, my app would have been outdated the moment it hit the App Store. When I conceived of Bistro Bash, it was spring 2013, and iOS 6 was the current operating system. Apple released iOS 7 in fall 2013, and it was a dramatic overhaul of the operating system and design. The design changed from textured in six to seven's flat, clean, and simple aesthetic. My mock-ups were immediately out of date the moment seven went online. If production had started and the layout had been fully designed, I would have needed thousands of dollars to update the visuals. Make sure you are up-to-date with recent software rumors or press releases pertaining to the device your app is being built on. Most likely, your developer will be aware of any upcoming design changes.

    If you do not understand what I am talking about, there is a great article on arstechnica.com by Andrew Cunningham titled "Death to Textures: iOS 6 and iOS 7 Compared in Pictures." I highly recommend you check it out. You will quickly understand the vigilance needed to stay atop changing trends.

FLEXIBILITY

    Assuming this is your first app project, trust the experience of your development team. More than likely, the people working on your app have been making mobile apps since Apple launched the App Store in 2008. Some of these developers were probably making web-based apps before that. Needless to say, their experience trumps yours. Do not start your app's production with a cocky or stubborn attitude with firm biases and convictions about your idea. As your app enters production, the core of your app's idea will be tested. Be flexible with your developer. Understand your concept, and know how you want your product to work, but let the developer guide you.

BE PREPARED

    Kelly Graver is a product designer at SnapMobile, a design agency that makes apps for an affordable flat fee. Located in Chicago, this design agency promises a MVP in just four weeks. By using components built for past projects, SnapMobile accelerates the development process. SnapMobile wants its clients' MVPs released quickly to gather feedback and iterate.

    Because of his mobile development background, I asked Kelly how educated an entrepreneur should be about technical topics. During an app's production, there will be lingo and terminology used by developers that may sound like a foreign language. "You should at least do your due diligence on the tools or techniques your development team will use on the app," said

Kelly. Although he says learning to code is not the answer, Kelly emphasizes entrepreneurs should have a certain level of confidence about what is being discussed. A baseline knowledge of technical topics prevents your idea from being steamrolled. It keeps a certain amount of your personal ownership involved in the project.

TECH STACK

When Bistro Bash entered production, I didn't have the slightest idea about tech stacking. Being technically illiterate will not derail your project, but you should at least attempt to acquaint yourself with basic terms. I believe a broad understanding of tech stacking is sufficient. As vice president of engineering at Dom & Tom, Danny Saad was a natural choice to discuss technical topics. Dom & Tom has come a long way since Danny quit his regular job to become the company's first employee. Today, Dom & Tom has offices in New York, Chicago, and Los Angeles. Since 2014, they have made Inc.'s 5000 List of Fastest Growing Companies in the United States. Dom & Tom has created over 100 native mobile apps including Priceline's first flight booking app. A native app is a program that has been developed for a specific platform such as iOS or Android. Their impressive portfolio includes clients such as Bloomberg, the Emmys, and Saban Brands.

PC Magazine defines a tech stack as "a set of software that provides the infrastructure for a computer." This will include the operating system, related support programs, and all runtime environments necessary to support the application.

Danny explained the development team will typically define all aspects of the stack they want to use and ultimately decide what is appropriate. "This typically includes the programming language, database technology, server software, client libraries, server technology, operating systems, among other elements," said Danny. He mentioned there are multiple factors that need to be considered. Besides costs, other factors include: the nature of the application being built, performance, and developer domain knowledge and experience.

Danny believes choosing a stack is important but not the most critical factor. "As a startup, use what makes sense and is inexpensive for you. If you ever have that 20, 30, or 40 million user base you typically have a revenue stream at that point to redo and build whatever fancy technology you want. The point is not to build [a first version] to last twenty years. Prove the product and create user retention that generates revenue so you can reinvest and upgrade your platforms."

UNDERSTANDING APIs

Hashrocket was an early adopter of Ruby on Rails, a framework that allows developers to build web-based applications. Today, Hashrocket is a leader in this space and boasts popular clients such as Brad's Deals, Vanderbilt University, and Aetna. Jack Christensen bills himself as a jack-of-all-trades at Hashrocket. He is an active member of the Rails community and has spoken at Windy City Rails, a Chicago Ruby on Rails conference. Naturally, our conversation was heavy on technical lingo.

Unless you are building an app that will not connect to the Internet whatsoever, one or more APIs will be needed to construct your app. An API is an application programming interface. Jack describes an API as "a protocol or language for one computer to talk to another or for one software on one computer to talk to software on another." For instance, if your mobile app uses Google Maps' data to find a business address, your app will communicate with Google Maps' API. Their API allows certain data from Google Maps to be accessible from the Internet.

Before software engineering commences, ask your developer which APIs your app will be communicating with. You want an API that is stable and can reliably store your data. "For somebody who is non-technical, the general rule of thumb for choosing a tech stack and API is to choose the most popular thing there is. You may have specific technical needs that may limit your options in some matter, but barring that go with whatever is most popular," said Jack. Popular APIs provided by Twitter, Microsoft, and Amazon are less likely to be removed from the Internet. These companies are incentivized to keep developers happy because they want people interacting with their content. Popular or widely adopted APIs will also have an abundance of documentation and support for developers to reference. This will make your development team's job easier.

Popular APIs are also less likely to go out of business. If you are dealing with an API hosted by a startup or new company, you may want to do your own research. Find out what is being said about that company in the news, on Facebook, or on Twitter. Companies that are trying to be acquired can be a risk; they may not be able to provide services indefinitely. Jack mentioned building a business on a third-party API is fine if your interests coincide, but your business can crumble if they close shop and pull their software from the Internet. Also, APIs hosted by larger companies are less likely to have problems. You want stability knowing that your app will always be online when you need it. Lakeview Labs refers to APIs as the "engine to your app," so make sure you are aware of the technology powering your future business.

BYE-BYE BISTRO BASH

Unfortunately, I know exactly why Jack from Hashrocket is concerned about startup APIs. All the data related to my ingredients, wrong answers, and dishes in Bistro Bash were hosted in the cloud at Parse. Parse was a rising star on the iOS development scene for several years and was acquired by Facebook for $85 million during 2013. Reportedly, Parse powered over 600,000 apps. During 2016, it was announced Facebook would shut down Parse in January 2017. All apps had to migrate their data to new services, or it would be wiped out when the cloud service shut down. However, Facebook was mum about specifics on why it was shutting it down. Bistro Bash was completely dependent on Parse to work. Parse going offline was the final blow to my app. I did not have any additional capital to migrate the data. Today, all that remains of Bistro Bash is the code itself.

Fortunately for most developers, Facebook gave developers more than a year to migrate their content and provided instructions to do so. Companies like Facebook can afford to give developers some adequate heads-up, but a startup swiftly closing their doors forever may not leave you with options. Your business could be wiped out overnight if you are completely dependent on the API.

DESIGN SPRINTS

Designs sprints were invented and popularized by Google Ventures. In a nutshell, design sprints are a simplified process that accelerates the development of a product. Within five days, an entrepreneur will have their idea prototyped and tested. The general time frame looks like this:

Day 1: Map the problem and put the idea into context

Day 2: Brainstorm and sketch out solutions

Day 3: Explore the best idea and begin design

Day 4: Build a cut-and-dry clickable prototype

Day 5: Test the product

Firms or developers may perform design sprints during discovery or other early stages of production. A design sprint is a cost-effective way to validate your idea before jumping into the expensive development process. Not only will it validate your idea, but it might also prevent you from creating an unneeded or useless app. Usually, you do not have to make any long-term commitments when you engage in a design sprint.

Most developers will offer a relatively cheap package to conduct a week of design sprints. If you cannot afford to produce an entire project, this is a good place to start. A design sprint output is usually a clickable prototype. At the end of the sprint, the developer will usually get the clickable prototype in front of your intended audience to gauge initial reactions.

CLICKABLE PROTOTYPE

All the founders and serial entrepreneurs I met with were eager to discuss their thoughts on untechnical people making apps, and Chris Pautsch, the founder of KeyLimeTie, was no exception. Like most app developers, Chris has had multiple clients shocked by the cost of their app. Most companies or early startups cannot afford to plunge all their capital to test a hypothetical idea. I had encountered a variety of strange developer names, but the name KeyLimeTie reverberated with me the most. It turns out Chris's first company's name was too generic to the point it lost them business. He owned a consulting firm called ConsultUs and had a hard time earning business with large companies when their competitors had more unique names. Somehow, Chris decided on KeyLimeTie when he started his development firm. Hence, you may want to think about a clever name for your app. KeyLimeTie has been making apps since 2010 and has built apps for Lava Lamp, AAA, and Allstate. Although Chris is both a developer and designer, nowadays he is mainly the big-picture guy and project manager.

Chris believes clickable prototypes are a necessity. A clickable prototype, sometimes referred to as a clickable mock-up, mimics the user flow your app will have. User flows are the screens a user must encounter to complete a task in the app. Besides using the prototype to gauge interest in the idea, clickable prototypes have other benefits.

Chris says people continuously underestimate the number of screens needed in their app. "Customers come in and say they have a super simple app idea that only requires a few screens for the app to function. We start walking them through the process. There's a login screen, registration, confirm your password, change your password, and forgot your password screen. Right there is a minimum of five screens and we haven't even got to what your app does," said Pautsch. "Making them go through the clickable prototype exercise forces them to think about all the screens. Making them go through that effort will actually force consolidation of screens and features."

Ask every studio how much it would cost to create a clickable prototype. Some developers make black-and-white clickable prototypes for free. They can be used effectively to raise capital and are an affordable tool to examine the functionality of your app before they are built. After seeing your clickable prototype, you may decide the app is not worth creating, or maybe it will evolve into a better project. The latter is usually the case.

PROJECT MANAGERS

Assuming your app is built by a third party, you will be assigned a project manager. After your engagement has been finalized and development has commenced, your project manager will be the person you coordinate with most frequently. Project managers are essential to getting your app developed on time and under budget. It is important to maintain a healthy relationship with them.

Heather Brown has spent her career in Chicago helping orchestrate digital projects for some of the world's most well-known brands: Motorola, Harpo Studios, Verizon, Kraft, and Sears. Like many in the app universe, Heather also dabbles in other ventures. Heather is also cofounder of both Bughouse and the Windy City Digital Project Managers. Today, she is the director of project management at Eight Bit Studios. Heather believes that communication is key to keeping the relationship stable and moving the project in the right direction. Your project manager should be judged by how informed you are throughout the entire process. "A client should know at all times what's going on with their project in the upcoming week, the items the developers are supposed to deliver, and what the client is personally responsible for," explained Heather. "The client should also be cognizant of where the budget stands and potential upcoming risks." To make fluid communication a priority, Heather believes project managers and clients should try to have one-on-one meetings aside from the normal project status updates.

However, this is not a one-sided relationship. You do not throw all the work on your project manager. Communication needs to be reciprocal. Do not just open your texts or emails and forget to respond. "Projects managers expect clients to be responsible for their to-dos throughout development. Clients should make themselves available to answer questions, discuss the project, and help the project manager guide their vision," said Heather. This is another scenario where time commitment should be a factor in your decision to make an app. Even during development, you will be required to make important decisions and provide guidance to your project managers. Very little assumptions are made during development without the input of the client.

Your project manager should be your best friend throughout the process. However, do not go over their heads. It may seem innocent, but never email or contact any of the engineers or designers working on your app without looping your project manager in first. Although your intentions might be innocent, it violates normal operating procedures.

THE USUAL PROCESS

Most developers pitch a unique production process. Although the process is not uniform across the board, there are several main pillars found at every studio. Unfortunately, it would be impossible to highlight every studio's strategy, so I morphed them into several points:

1. Discovery
2. User experience and design
3. Engineering
4. Test
5. Repeat

Please remember the process is hardly linear. Discovery might overlap with the "user experience and design" stages. Design and engineering may be done simultaneously. Do not be alarmed if your developer refers to each stage with different terminology. Understanding the typical process will help you make an informed decision on who makes your app.

DISCOVERY

It is important you fully understand your developer's discovery stage. Each team has a unique approach to discovery with its own value proposition. This stage is the foundation of your app's development and crucial to your app's early success. In most cases, the discovery stage will incorporate elements of a design sprint.

The initial phase is to proof the idea. Here they will want to prototype your product, conduct their own research, and validate. Usually their prototyping will be no different than what you bring to them. Maybe it will be a clickable prototype. Heather Brown, director of project management at Eight Bit Studios, says discovery allows all stakeholders to take a holistic view of the idea. Essentially, holes or gaps in the idea are filled in, and the larger picture becomes more vivid.

During discovery, the idea will morph into something different, usually something better. Your idea may be very creative but still raw. A responsible studio will want the idea to have legs in the market. High-flying ideas are thrown around the room. The design studio and I would continuously be throwing out whacky, explosive ideas onto the whiteboard. You should embrace all the ideas thrown around in this brainstorming session, but do not forget about the items you nix. Throughout the life of Bistro Bash, people would tell me all the time what I should do or put into the app. Very few that I heard were completely original ideas; many ideas were thrown out during the brainstorm for a good reason. Some potential features for your app may seem simple but are expensive to implement. Make sure your mission-critical ideas are implemented before the fluff is. Stay focused on your idea's main crux or the problem it is solving. Several crucial questions, such as the ones below, will need to be answered during this phase:

- What is this app about?
- What is the core or defining feature?
- Why would people use it?
- Why would people keep using it?

The answers to these questions will dictate the project going forward. Your idea could have multiple features and niches, but it may not need to. Ask yourself if you really need all those extra screens and features. You want users engaging with your product through as few screens as possible. Figure out the difference between nice-to-have and need-to-have features. Save the nice-to-have features for later. In a studio situation, project managers will type notes quickly on a laptop while you and the rest of the team brainstorm. Many of the nice-to-have features will be put aside and hopefully arise on another day. Think about your favorite apps as they look today, and then think about how they looked when you originally started using them. Most likely, the app you use today looks vastly different than how it did when you first started using it with one exception: the main part of the app functions the same. "Scale down your product tremendously for the initial release," said Danny Saad, vice president of engineering at Dom & Tom. Project manager Cyrus Kiani of CitrusBits mentioned people forget that their favorite apps evolved over time. "Clients want their app fully loaded. Popular apps like Instagram have been refined over several years. These apps added features because users slowly acclimated to their product," said Cyrus.

"Clients building something from scratch have been really successful when they have a discussion about what they want versus what is actually possible," said Jake Worth, a developer at Hashrocket.

For Bistro Bash, the main feature, or crux, was the game. That should have been my only focus, but I wanted too much, too quickly. I wanted the ability to share scores with friends over social media, power-ups, and in-app purchases. I was completely wrong and misinformed. My first version should have only been the game and nothing else. First, it would have saved money. Two, it would have allowed more time and resources allotted to testing and tweaking the game after initial feedback. Know what is important, and get that built as soon as possible.

A popular example most people should be familiar with is Snapchat. In the beginning, Snapchat was only for sending disappearing pictures. What was originally thought to be a fad turned out to be a billion-dollar hit in the making. Snapchat continuously improved upon that main feature, but it remains the core feature of the app. Today, Snapchat allows users to also send videos, share videos or pictures on a public timeline, and view the news. Chief executive and founder Evan Spiegel may have always wanted these other features in his grand vision, but he knew what the app's core was from the beginning. Although the scope of Snapchat has broadly expanded, everything that followed became possible because the core feature was a success.

Developers want their clients to reach their market as soon as possible. If the core of the app works, they will usually push for the app to be released.

The discovery stage is the foundation of all that is to follow. Hence, every stakeholder for your project should have their opinion heard. Stakeholders include the engineers, UX team, designers, researchers, investors, or whoever else will be involved moving forward. All stakeholders should be involved during discovery to provide context for decision-making. Besides discovery's importance in laying out the vision, it is an important alignment period. Everybody working on the project should understand their role and contribution. As the creator, you should know who is doing what. This is where everybody buys into that vision, and the real work begins.

After the discovery stage concludes, your project's scope should be trimmed significantly. Usually your project manager should present you with a new agreed-upon list of deliverables and goals. For discovery to be considered a success, this stage should accomplish two things: culminate in a smaller scope and the scope should result in a product you will be happy with. Nailing this and being happy with your smaller scope is essential to prevent scope creep. Almost every developer I spoke to warned me that scope creep often tore through an app's production budget. Scope creep is the continuous growth of a project's scope. Also, understanding that your app will not initially look like you envisioned is crucial to preventing scope creep.

DESIGN AND USER EXPERIENCE

Both design and user experience (UX) go together. One cannot work without the other, and neither can your app. Consumers spy with their eyes, so a beautiful design is important, but functionality is just as essential.

The foundation of both UX and design are the wireframes. Although you may start seeing wireframes in discovery, they will certainly appear in design and UX. Wireframes will reveal all the screens in your app with notes explaining the function of each screen. It allows clients to walk through their app's interface. Hashrocket compared wireframes to storyboards that provide a visual representation of what is being built. Heather Brown from Eight Bit Studios compared it to a blueprint. Both comparisons are accurate. Wireframes will inform design and user experience. For example, a wireframe might indicate you need to enter your birth month to enter the app. A designer and UX expert will try to make that function visually striking, but easy to use. They may realize a drop-down option is more appropriate than a keyboard to manually type the month and day. "People often do not think about how they interact with an app," said Jack Christensen, a developer at Hashrocket. "I want a high-level blueprint so we know what to build."

The output of the design and UX will be fully designed app pages. "If people are dying to get on your product, design and other details that might matter to you, won't matter to your users. They just want to access your app," said Vidal Ekechukwu, a developer from Hashrocket. Do not get all fussy if you are not blown away by the design. If the design is on par with current design trends, your app looks good enough.

ENGINEERING

This is where your app will come to life. Although developers may start working on your app during discovery, most of the programming will take place after the design and UX. To keep it simple, the software engineering of your app will be broken into two parts: front end and back end. The front end refers to the components manipulated by the users that brings your user interface to life and makes it functional. The engineering during this phase makes the app's data usable and accessible to your future customers.

During back end, the data layer design and the logic required to bring the data to the user is programmed. "Most of the development work in the back end happens in database terminals and text files, and is focused on design, security, and performance," said Jake Worth of Hashrocket. Anything created in back-end development will never be seen by the user.

TEST

Regardless of all your idea validation, design sprints, and hypotheticals, you will never know how users interact with your app or where it fits in the marketplace until you get it in their hands. By the way, testing does not mean just pressing buttons and looking at all the pretty screens in the app. Test users should be interacting with the main function of your app. Sure, they can give you feedback on the design and their opinions on secondary features, but you need to know what they think about the crux of your app.

When you test your app, do not just show it to close friends and family. People in your close inner circle will be overwhelmed with excitement for you, and their feedback will most likely be biased. Focus on showing your app to the intended audience.

REPEAT

Your development process never truly ends! If development for an app ends, then that app is no longer being serviced and is out of business. The apps on your phone are constantly being updated. Whether designs are being updated or bugs are being fixed, apps are in a continuous state of development. Most new development is spurred by user reaction and testing. Thus, new development is usually a direct response to consumer sentiment. If you are further developing your app to meet the needs of your customers, you are probably in a good spot and should be happy you have that problem.

How to Succeed:

- Ensure your developer is up-to-date with developer account protocols and design trends.
- Trust your team's development experience.
- Familiarize yourself with technical lingo before your app begins production.
- Be knowledgeable about the technology powering your app.
- Design sprints and clickable prototypes are a cheap alternative to building and testing a functioning app.
- Listen to your project manager and build a strong relationship with them.
- Development for an app never ends.

9

THE FIRST VERSION

Turning an idea into an app can happen very quickly once a developer gets their hands on it. Therefore, you need to be prepared for the first version's release far ahead of time and keep your objectives realistic. "A typical project is often developed in four to six months. Some projects are done faster and some can take longer. I generally advise companies not to take too long because you don't want to spend too much time developing a product without getting customer feedback and validation," said Greg Raiz, CEO of Raizlabs. Remember, your app will be far from perfect. The first release of your app can be a bit daunting. The best advice: do not be afraid. Sometimes, entrepreneurs may get cold feet or afraid of putting their app out there. After months of hyping an app to friends and family, the first version may initially feel or look underwhelming. As long as your app functions properly and it provides a true benefit to its users, your fears are completely misplaced. Be proud of what you accomplished, and get that app on as many screens as possible.

Do not wait until your app is already completed before making moves. Marketing, advertising, and scaling beyond your initial user base will eventually become priorities. None of these skills or opportunities will just fall into your lap.

KEEP IT SMALL

Jake Worth, a West Point graduate and Iraq War veteran, taught himself to code after the military. He focuses primarily on web-based applications and is a developer at Hashrocket. He and another developer, Jack Christensen, were interviewed together. They both discussed common mistakes entrepreneurs make on their first version. "The majority of companies I have encountered grew slowly into a profitable business," said Jake. "This theory that you're going to launch and get this firehose of users flooding your app is very rare."

Jake and Jack believe founders make expensive errors by wrongly anticipating an immediate avalanche of users upon release. "It's expensive to build an app anticipating millions of users when you may only get thousands," remarked Jack. Personally, I think thousands of users can even be a stretch for most apps on an initial rollout. "The biggest problem isn't something gets attention and it crashes, it's that it just never gets attention."

"Anticipating this need for great scalability upfront is not needed," added Jake. "Scalability is always a concern of developers. They want to know how their product will respond if it is overwhelmed with traffic."

"That's a problem most founders do not have to worry about," laughed Jack. "Most projects do not fail based on technical reasons, its business concerns." Entrepreneurs should want their app to fail from being overloaded with users—it's a problem most are not fortunate to have. Your focus should be on your business proposition and effectively executing that strategy.

Per clutch.co's January 2015 survey of app-development studios, the most time-consuming segment of development was related to scalability. By not worrying about your product's ability to scale off the bat, your app can enter the market quicker. "The earlier you launch, the earlier you can get feedback. Maybe the feedback you are going to get is that your app currently sucks. In this case, you can cut your losses early or change direction," explained Jack. "Launch early and launch often."

USERS

Your initial objective should be acquiring and retaining users, not revenue. Babies need to crawl before they can walk. Apps need users before they can make money. You do not need a million users from around the globe to start earning revenue. Believe it or not, any stable number of users is a fantastic start.

Hence, you do not need a global rollout strategy. Focus on acquiring repeat users in a certain geographic area. Once you figure out the type of consumer using your app, it will be easy to expand.

Once you have a stable user base, it is important there is incoming revenue. Either these users are paying to use your app or another company is paying to market to people interacting with your app. Both are sufficient to justify expansion; however, paying users is the most valuable source of revenue in most scenarios. A stable user base of any size and a real stream of revenue will get you all the funding needed to scale into new markets.

Hoping that you will stumble upon a user base is not a strategy. It may seem simple enough, but finding genuine, repeat users is difficult. It can be the most frustrating part of the app's life. "Releasing an app is not the hard part, user acquisition and retention is by far more difficult," remarked Danny Saad, vice president of engineering at Dom & Tom. "We have seen it a million times where a client has a product, but they cannot get anybody to use it. They cannot reach eyeballs."

EMPOWER WITH TECHNOLOGY

Most college students land their first post-graduation jobs from an internship, but few are elevated from intern to a management position like Jonathan Reilly. Fortunately for Jonathan, DRYV is an on-demand laundry startup competing in a challenging industry. As is often the case with startups, executive and management positions depend less on years of experience and more on action that produces results.

However, Jonathan had made his fair share of mistakes along the way. One of his earlier mistakes was placing too much emphasis on vanity metrics. Vanity metrics include items such as registered users, downloads, and page views. An early strategy he rolled out as an intern involved him handing out promotional cards and collecting people's e-mails using a landing page. "This was great for sign-ups and building an email list, but the conversion of people creating an order was very low," remarked Jon. As his e-mail list was growing, first-time orders were lagging. Jonathan began to execute a new strategy that involved the same tactic but solely in corporate lobbies or residential buildings. Fewer people were engaging Jonathan, but conversions went up. "Almost every person who signed up would create an order and I quickly realized that I initially had been going after the wrong demographic and focusing on the wrong metric."

He also spoke a bit about DRYV's operations and scaling. Through trial and error, DRVY survived while others, such as Washio, perished. When Jonathan first joined as an intern, DRYV was doing the pickups and deliveries while outsourcing the cleaning to a large plant. This was neither scalable nor cost effective. DRYV soon began the transition to becoming a technology platform that empowered cleaners to do pickups and delivery. Since the transition, DRVY has evolved and now includes cleaners in multiple cities that use lockers, doorman pickups, and both route and on-demand pickups. "One of the biggest mistakes that can be made is not recognizing the cost of on-demand [services]. Fast growing companies have fallen because they did not recognize the cost of multiple drivers on the road at once." Competing in the on-demand space can be challenging to provide affordable services without raising the price for consumers.

DRYV originally serviced only several neighborhoods in Chicago but has since expanded to other cities. Today, DRYV can be found in Chicago, Detroit, New Orleans, Indianapolis, San Francisco, Grand Rapids, and Minneapolis. "It can be tough handling support tickets and operations when scaling into a new city," said Jonathan. "To appropriately scale, you need to think about how you can empower your partners to handle some of the workload without having to hire new people. For example, if a cleaner misplaces an item we cannot physically go retrieve it like we can here in Chicago." He credits their forward-thinking development team for solving some of these problems like misplaced items. They built tracking features for cleaners to track down which order was with which driver. Because of this feature, fewer items were being misplaced. This mitigated the need for more support to be hired by DRYV.

As the final thought, Jonathan advised on-demand or "Uber for X" companies to build features that improve the process for both consumers and partners. Be sure to speak with stakeholders before implementing an update because a feature made for your customers may be hell for your partners.

REDEFINING FOOD DELIVERY

Sterling Douglass's first app, Nyx, crashed and burned. After talking with Sterling for several minutes, it became apparent he had learned many of the unappealing truths. Sterling was working as an actuary at Willis Towers Watson, a global consulting firm. He was fed up with the corporate life and started brainstorming ideas he could build into a company. "If you have an entrepreneurial itch, you need to dive in and embrace the pressure," said Sterling. Sterling decided to build Nyx, an app that allowed customers in a crowded bar to order and pay for drinks on their phone. Lacking sufficient technical skills to build Nyx on his own, he found a self-taught cofounder who developed most of the app. The Nyx team then hired a third party to construct the data and payment infrastructure. Nyx did not start selling their services to bars until after the product launched. As a result, they had very little knowledge of what their customers wanted (similar to my own experience with Bistro Bash). After six months of operations, Nyx shut down.

Instead of sulking and dragging out his failed app, Sterling shuttered Nyx and formed a second technology company that quickly roared to life. As Sterling was selling Nyx to bars, he realized their workers wasted a lot of time transferring orders from their delivery platform to their point-of-sale system. There was no uniform integration platform that a restaurant could use to bridge the two. A restaurant's point-of-sale system would be a cash register or another computer terminal where orders are entered, payment is received, and the customer is given a receipt. Most restaurants allow customers to place an order for delivery using apps like GrubHub, UberEATS, or Eat24. Because of Nyx, Sterling met Brian Duncan, and the two decided to tackle this widespread problem head-on. Chowly was born.

They quickly succeeded where others had failed. Several major technology companies had tried to merge third-party delivery apps with point-of-sale systems but were unsuccessful. "The problems were inherent in the market, there are over 450 point-of-sale systems in the United States," explained Sterling. He mentioned that other technology companies had tried to hire consulting companies or build integration software internally, but red tape and inadequate resources always stopped the projects in their tracks. If a restaurant changed what was on their point-of-sale system, they would also need to update the ordering apps. Keeping up with all the changes was too much content management and busy work for some established companies. Chowly saw this opportunity, and it was theirs for the taking.

Chowly's developer, another cofounder, started development immediately. As a startup, they were able to iterate five to ten times a day and deploy new code constantly. There was no red tape or corporate bureaucracy. "We formed Chowly on November 19, 2015 and we had our first paying client by December 18. We were able to get market validation in less than 30 days," described Sterling. "The power of being able to iterate so quickly is what allowed it to grow and evolve into a great content management tool." Sterling was just cold-calling and walking into random restaurants. Unlike Nyx, Chowly was iterating and selling their product constantly. In the first five months, they were doubling their sales growth every month. Chowly installs software on a restaurant's point-of-sale system and connects it to their delivery apps. Each has a separate menu, so Chowly links those two together. "We call this menu mapping. The mappings take time to build. For example, we make sure a hot dog on the delivery app is a hot dog on the point-of-sale system," explained Sterling. For their first iteration, Chowly did not even have modifications available. It took hours upon hours for the team to do it manually. "That was not a scalable product, but that didn't matter. We just needed our system to input orders." Chowly proves that neither complex nor scalable technology is needed in your first release. App entrepreneurs just need to release a product that works. How your first product works or whatever makes it tick should be of little concern to you. Sterling proclaims the first version was ugly and hardly worked, but hardly was enough. With a functioning product, Chowly streamlined the ordering process for restaurants. Their quick, upward trajectory was fascinating. "One of the reasons Chowly was so good at getting off the ground was because we are scrappy. We are scrappy at sales, scrappy with operations and our technology, and scrappy with client communications," said Sterling. He advises future app entrepreneurs to take as many shortcuts as they can as long as they are still providing value to customers. Today, Sterling is the chief executive officer of Chowly, and he owes a lot of his success to Nyx. "I learned more in six months building Nyx than I did in four years of college," explained Sterling. If you want to emulate Sterling and Chowly's success, remember it is okay to fail. Each failure or setback will bless you with priceless experience. Apply every lesson quickly and build on that.

"Eventually, we plateaued and couldn't bootstrap any longer." With only three people, Chowly had accelerated quickly and it needed its first capital injection. Several venture-capital firms and other individuals provided funds for Chowly to expand. As of March 2017, Chowly has fourteen employees, and its services are used in over thirty states. Their technology can be integrated with over 170 different online ordering platforms. I asked Sterling what his final goal was for Chowly, and he replied: "To take over the world." Like many successful entrepreneurs, Sterling wants to establish an empire. He might get his wish. Chowly is currently expanding into Canada, Europe, and the Asia-Pacific region. Not bad for a company that rose from the ashes of a failed app and the hustle of only three people.

PIVOT

Negative feedback should not be a cause for panic. Embrace all the feedback you get! The only mistake you can make regarding feedback is ignoring it entirely. If the initial reaction to your app suggests your current strategy is not working, you have two choices: cut your losses or pivot. There is nothing wrong with pivoting—it means you are learning and adapting to the marketplace. Just, please, do not pivot like I did.

When I first pivoted Bistro Bash, I threw on a fresh coat of paint and added more pointless features—a horrible idea. I did not even consider changing the literal center of the app: the gameplay itself. Basically, I decided to update the designs after only five weeks of release. The designs should have been the least of my concerns. Had users been complaining about the designs, then changing the user interface and designs would have made sense. Not a single person complained about the design. The second major change I made was changing the game from one large level to thirty smaller levels. After learning from developers across the country, I can pinpoint this pivot as another point where I went wrong. I should have been refining the gameplay and trying to make it more fun, not adding unneeded features.

People would always pitch me new features to add to Bistro Bash, but nobody ever suggested changing the gameplay. It was a mistake focusing solely on features. Talking with developers has taught me a valuable lesson: nobody uses apps for the extra features. Good features are only ancillary to great apps. Your app is not the sum of its parts. If you do decide to pivot your app, pivot the crux of it. Wherever you expect your users to spend the most time should be most susceptible to pivots.

Reading this book and doing everything right does not guarantee your idea or your app will be a success. There is always the possibility your app will not connect with users. And that is okay. The important thing is you know when to walk away. A true entrepreneur does not view this as quitting. A failed app may hurt your ego, but get over yourself. Some of the most notable innovators and pioneers were shaped by their early failures in both life and entrepreneurship. Time is perhaps an entrepreneur's greatest asset, and you should waste none of it pushing an app that is already dead. Like many, I made the mistake of having an unhealthy love affair with my first venture, and it was hard to walk away from. This needs to be avoided and there are several signs to look for that will indicate that the game is up. Cyrus Kiani, project manager at CitrusBits, stated there are several red flags that indicate it could be time to throw in the towel:

1. A competitor in your space has a better product and you lack funding for app updates.
2. Your product has become irrelevant based on the current demand.
3. If you have better ideas, sometimes holding on to a failing app will prevent you from exploring the new opportunities.

If user acquisition growth is slow, declining, or non-existent, these are stout indications your app is heading in the wrong direction. Once initial momentum for your app has stalled, a lack of funding can strangle any chance of a meaningful pivot. Second, it may be worth it to invest those funds elsewhere, like a new app idea. Neither new features nor shiny designs can save an unpopular product or service. Do not use anecdotal evidence to counter the data that suggests your app is becoming irrelevant. A few random users that enjoy your app may not be sufficient evidence to continue the business.

Steve Polacek, the cofounder of Eight Bit Studios has seen apps sputter out for multiple reasons, but thinks people should not throw in the towel until they have investigated thoroughly. "If you're not getting downloads, is it because your app sucks or you're not marketing it effectively? If you're getting downloads, but people aren't engaging, find out where they are falling off," explained Steve. "If you still care enough about the purpose behind the app, you'll keep going. You'll take everything you've learned and figure out a better way to accomplish your goals. If you don't care enough to keep going, then you need to find a new problem to solve."

It's important to differentiate between bumps in the road and a dead end. Bumps in the road are going to be encountered along the entire journey—those are the challenges that can and will be addressed. A dead end is when you summon the courage to walk away and apply your raw experiences to something better. "If you decide to pivot your ideas, you now have new lessons and experiences to help you become even more successful," exclaimed Joe Musselman, CEO of The Honor Foundation.

"I believed in the product with every ounce of my soul up until the very end," recalled Sterling Douglass about his failed app Nyx. "My cofounder sent me a letter of resignation and my original developer was going back to school. With no coding people on staff, I knew I was not set up for success. I laid down on my bedroom floor and stared at the ceiling for a few hours with a pretty blank mind." After speaking to his brother, Sterling cleared his mind and started focusing on Chowly. Once Chowly nabbed its first paying customer, all that passion once reserved for Nyx had migrated to his new venture. "I think an entrepreneur's ability to get punched in the face and continue to get up is a defining characteristic of what we do."

Even in your worst-case scenario, at the very least you will be walking away with highly transferable skills and your next venture will benefit. "You can't avoid failing, but if you're going to fail…fail quickly and embrace that," said Mark Rickmeier, CEO of Table XI.

EMBARRASSING

Too many entrepreneurs hold on for too long. I was one of them. Until the end, I had no coherent strategy, and I could not see the path forward. After two years, it became increasingly painful to discuss Bistro Bash. When friends brought it up, I would secretly cringe. When you live with a problem for too long, you care less about solving it and more about ridding yourself of the burden.

All my friends and family knew I created Bistro Bash, but when reality set in that the app was a dud, it became extremely hard to talk about. I would quickly change the subject if somebody brought the topic up or asked how it was doing.

On the other hand, I was still trying to find a spot where Bistro Bash could work and continued to pivot the product. Nevertheless, it was rejected time and time again. I allocated no capital to pay myself for my time and never took a cent from the funds. As a college student, I passed up multiple job opportunities and internships. If I had taken these positions, I would have had no time to work on Bistro Bash. As a student juggling part-time jobs, classwork, and Bistro Bash, it seemed as if I was never living in the present. Your personal and public sentiment about your app should be on or near the same level. Once there is a significant shift in this sentiment, it is time to re-examine what you are doing.

By treating an app as a business from the beginning, you will outline goals and understand the time and mindset needed. Do yourself a favor and assess your project every two months. If the app has not improved, walk away or prepare to walk away. Do not run in circles, as I did for two years. Continuously assess your progress and avoid the point where your app becomes painful to talk about. Avoiding the unappealing truth that your app has failed will not change the outcome. Do not be afraid to accept defeat and try again another day.

How to Succeed:

- Preparation for your app's release should begin long before initial development concludes.
- Get your app released as soon as possible.
- Your first version may be underwhelming—don't let this bother you.
- Your app won't fail because of technical problems. It will fail because it's a bad idea or is being executed poorly.
- You do not need a global rollout strategy.
- Build the bare minimum needed to provide your users value.
- React appropriately to both positive and negative feedback.

- If your app is failing, discover what people do not like about it.

10

THE NEW FRONTIER

The app market is constantly changing as apps are paired with new innovations, exciting trends are adapted, and new gadgets are released. Thus, it made sense to look toward the horizon and find out what the experts had to say.

BEYOND THE SCREEN

When I interviewed Steve Polacek, he was a robot—literally. I interviewed several individuals from Eight Bit Studios, and Steve was the second interview. When my first interview concluded, Heather told me she would send Steve in. Then, Steve came in…sort of. A Double 2 robot rolled into the room streaming a live feed of Steve projected on an iPad. Steve was working from home that day and he was controlling the robot's movements, and it was like he was in the room with me. It seemed more authentic than a FaceTime or Skype conversation.

Eight Bit Studios, a known early adopter of new technologies, is cofounded by Steve. Some of Polacek's former clients include Britney Spears, Aerosmith, Justin Timberlake, Hard Rock, NBA, and the WNBA. He believes great product design starts with empathy and ends with solving a problem. Naturally, I wanted Steve's opinion on the future of user experience and design. "For so long, digital design has been confined solely to the screen," said Steve. "[Virtual and augmented reality, Internet of things] break open the mold and there will be tons of exciting possibilities." However, Steve warns the new opportunities to integrate these technologies will increase the complexity and scope of a project.

"People will need to be more diligent about prioritizing what is important and exercise discipline," said Steve. For years, companies have had to choose between whether to release

Android, iOS, or both. These same companies now must juggle multiple app markets and new technologies. "Today, it is expected a company release an app on both iOS and Android. Now imagine you have all these other places you can be. It is important to remember who your customers are and what are the best ways to reach them."

FLESHING OUT DEPARTMENTS

Design studios have significant advantages over freelancers. Unlike freelancers, design studios have the resources and extra time to conduct their own research and development. Today, most studios are experimenting and tweaking with the new cutting-edge technology. To stay competitive, studios are getting ready for the new frontier so they can smoothly transition beyond the mobile screen. As new technologies are used less for fun and have more commercial utility, new ideas and clients will undoubtedly rush to build the next big thing.

"It has been surprising how huge Internet of things has been in our mobile department. We have built apps that analyze car engines and send reports to the phone for predicting engine failures. Another app we made automatically locks down a work station as a person walks away from their desk. The app will then unlock the station when the person returns," said Danny Saad, vice president of engineering at Dom & Tom. Besides the Internet of things, Danny believes augmented and mixed reality will make a sizable impact on daily lives in the next several years. To prepare, Dom & Tom has put together a virtual reality department.

Dom & Tom is not the only East Coast–based studio making moves into the future. Raizlabs in Boston is exploring machine learning, artificial intelligence, and chat bots. In 2014, Raizlabs was recognized in *Popular Science's* "Best of What's New" and won "Innovation of the Year" with SunSprite. SunSprite is a Bluetooth wearable device that tracks wearers' sunlight exposure. The device ran completely on solar energy. The devices fed data to a smartphone allowing wearers to examine their exposure information in real time.

Nate Schier, a founding partner of Sidebench, spoke about their experience tapping into the new frontier. In 2016, Sony Home Entertainment partnered with Sidebench to build a Ghostbuster's virtual reality experience on the Google Cardboard VR platform. Although Nate admits virtual reality is cool, it is still in its early stages and will still be several years before it makes a large impact on the average consumer.

Chris Pautsch, the CEO of KeyLimeTie, said larger companies will be the first to jump on the bandwagon with these technologies. "These new and innovative technologies are used to re-engage or contain existing user bases. Larger companies want something that is one-of-a-kind and differentiating. It is less about monetization and more about brand awareness," said Pautsch.

FLASHING LIGHTS

The L, Chicago's rapid transit system that rides both above and below the city, is known for the dark shadow it can cast over urban areas in the city. However, this distinguishing but sometimes ugly feature of the city will soon be brightened by a public art project powered by mobile technology. The Wabash Lights project hopes to transform the L infrastructure on Wabash Avenue "into a canvas for dynamic, interactive experience." This nonprofit company hopes to line colorful and vibrant neon LED lights beneath the L. I was fortunate enough to speak with Table XI, the development team responsible for bringing The Wabash Lights online. The project was initially made possible through Kickstarter and an investment by Table XI. "They had this idea to attach lights that were pressure and noise sensitive that could change color as the train passes overhead. [Wabash Avenue] is a dark, dingy place. It's not dangerous, it just looks creepy," said Table XI CEO Mark Rickmeier. They also wanted the public to be able to change the lights on their smartphones. Table XI and The Wabash Lights team worked together to create a public beta and verify it was possible to create. Together, they originally reconstructed the popular electronic game Simon to learn how the lights would react. Table XI proved that the technology needed to power the project was readily available.

Given his experience with The Wabash Lights and other Internet of things projects, Mark and Table XI are extremely bullish for the next frontier of app development. "A while ago, [developers] needed to know web technology, then mobile, but the really good developers today are thinking about hardware and hardware integrations," said Mark. He mentioned many of the developers at Table XI also have soldering kits at their workstations. In the coming years, many development studios will need to staff mechanical engineers to build and solder things. Understanding physics and building actual machines will be just as important as software.

The cost is finally coming down, and practical applications for many products, including augmented and virtual reality, are increasing. Mark believes these new technologies are going to integrate with people's lives more and more over the coming years. He is interested to see how design and user experience will change as voice commands replace user interfaces.

THE CAVEMAN PRINCIPLE

With the new frontier quickly approaching, it might seem that an app's days are numbered. Artificial intelligence, chat bots, and voice recognition might push our eyes away from the screen. In March 2017, *Futurism* published an article titled "Tech Giants Are Racing to Be the First to Develop 'The Last App'" by Benjamin Stecher. Companies like Google, Samsung, Microsoft, and Amazon are investing in technology to power personal digital assistants that can do everything and anything you want it to do. Because of personal assistants like Microsoft's Cortana and Apple's Siri, we may not need to interact with our phones or devices again.

Although we might use these intelligent personal assistants more often, they will not completely replace apps on a screen. Dr. Michio Kaku, a theoretical physicist and best-selling author, often speaks about "The Caveman Principle." As an esteemed futurist, Dr. Kaku believes the best way to predict the future is to look at our past. In his book *Physics of the Future*, Dr. Kaku explains human brains and personalities have changed little since modern humans emerged from African caves over 100,000 years ago. "If you gave [a caveman] a bath and a shave, put him in a three-piece suit, and then placed him on Wall Street, he would be indistinguishable from everyone else," wrote Kaku; he believes the desires of our primitive ancestors still trump our desire for technology. Our desires to touch and have a real tangible connection to our environment and others explain why so many predictions about the future never came true. For example, Kaku said the paperless office never came to be because we still prefer hard copies of files. "We instinctively don't trust the electrons floating in our computer screen, so we print our e-mails and reports, even when it's not necessary."

Other examples Dr. Kaku provides give weight to this theory. The Internet was predicted to make conventional media and entertainment obsolete. "Of course, the Internet has changed the entire media landscape, as media giants puzzle over how to earn revenue on the Internet. But it is not even close to wiping out TV, radio, and live theater. The lights of Broadway still glow as brightly as before." These gloomy predictions never came true.

As Dr. Kaku says, "One medium never annihilates a previous one but coexists with it." The same theory can be applied to apps. Virtual and augmented reality, artificial intelligence, chat bots, and Internet of things will not end the need for apps. In the near future, apps will coexist with these new technologies and take on new forms. The apps created in 2027 will look and function drastically different than apps from 2017. Nevertheless, apps will be more important in our lives and our reliance on them will only increase. The remaining question is: what app will you build?

ACKNOWLEDGEMENTS

Professor Patrick Murphy at DePaul University for being a guiding hand throughout the entire process.

Kyle Henry for helping craft the book's message and spring boarding ideas.

To twenty-eight individuals who lent me their time, experience, and insights. Without you, this book would not have been possible.

Thank you.

NOTES

Chapter 1

"Median cost range is between $37,913 and $171,450": Craigmile, Natalie. "Cost to Build a Mobile App: Survey." Clutch. Clutch, 30 Jan. 2015. Web.

How Do You Make Money When Less Than 1% of Apps are 'Financially Successful.': Caulderwood, Kathleen. "How Do You Make Money When Less Than 1% Of Apps Are 'Financially Successful'." International Business Times. IBT Media Inc., 14 Jan. 2014. Web.

"In 2013, Yahoo purchased Summly for $30 million": Luckerson, Victor. "Why Is That 17-Year-Old's $30 Million News App Even Legal?" Time. Time, 27 Mar. 2013. Web.

"The app launched in 2011… Actor Ashton Kutcher was among the early investors of Summly": Sandle, Paul. "Just Do It, Says Yahoo's Teen App Millionaire." Reuters. Thomson Reuters, 26 Mar. 2013. Web.

"D'Aloisio unveiled Yahoo News Digest, a clear improvement upon Summly": Dickey, Megan Rose. "Yahoo Is Finally Making Something Out of Summly, The Mobile App It Acquired From A 17-Year-Old Boy." Business Insider. Business Insider, 07 Jan. 2014. Web.

"App Annie, an analytics and market-data firm, estimates that the app market will exceed 284 billion downloads in 2020": App Annie. App Annie Mobile App Forecast: The Path to $100 Billion: Appannie.com. App Annie. Web.

"the mobile app market is highly competitive, but the economical upside can be great for the successful publishers": Svanberg, Johan. The Mobile Application Market (n.d.): n. pag. Web.

Chapter 2

"During September 2016 that they would be purging the App Store of outdated content": Apple. "App Store Improvements." Apple Developer. N.p., n.d. Web.

NOTES

In 2013, Google removed over 60,000 apps that were in the graveyard: Perez, Sarah. "Nearly 60K Low-Quality Apps Booted from Google Play Store in February, Points to Increased Spam-Fighting." TechCrunch. TechCrunch, 08 Apr. 2013. Web.

CNET Top Grossing iPhone Apps Ever: "Top 10 Grossing iPhone Apps Ever." CNET. N.p., n.d. Web.

<https://www.cnet.com/pictures/top-10-grossing-iphone-apps-ever-pictures/>.

"Apple announced in 2016 that Super Mario Bros… would finally be arriving on the App Store": Gilbert, Ben. "There's One Simple Reason Nintendo Is Bringing Super Mario to the IPhone First." Business Insider. Business Insider, 09 Sept. 2016. Web.

"Mobile users could opt-in for a notification alerting them the moment Super Mario Run hit the App Store": Perez, Sarah. "Apple's App Store Gets a "Notify" Button for Soon-to-launch apps." TechCrunch. TechCrunch, 07 Sept. 2016. Web.

"Two days before launch, twenty million iPhone users had signed up for the notification": Kharpal, Arjun. "Nintendo's 'Super Mario Run' on IOS Set to Gross $71 Million in First Month, Less than Half of 'Pokemon Go'." CNBC. CNBC, 08 Dec. 2016. Web.

"However, Super Mario Run only had 2.5 stars after 55,000+ reviews had been submitted": Davies, Chris. "Super Mario Run Players Are Slamming It with One-star Reviews." SlashGear. N.p., 16 Dec. 2016. Web.

"On December 17, the game peaked the charts of 138 countries. Before the year was over, the app had plummeted to only sixty-eight countries": Nakamura, Yuji. "Super Mario Run Loses Life on App Store Charts." Chicagotribune.com. N.p., 27 Dec. 2016. Web.

Chapter 4

"Today, Tinder boasts on its website that more than 10 billion matches have been made and there are over 1.4 billion swipes per day": https://www.gotinder.com/press

"Product Hunt features a page called "There's a Tinder for everything.":
https://www.producthunt.com/e/tinder-for-x

"In fact, mobile gaming revenue surpassed $40 billion in 2016":
Takahashi, Dean. "SuperData: Mobile Games Hit $40.6 Billion in 2016, Matching World Box Office Numbers." VentureBeat. N.p., 01 Feb. 2017. Web.

"Almost five years after its initial debut, it still consistently ranks around among the top-selling apps internationally": Cowley, Ric. "Candy Crush Saga Has Only Dropped out of the US App Store Top Ten Grossing Charts Twice in over Four Years." Pocketgamer.biz. N.p., 13 Apr. 2017. Web

"Per their 2015 annual report, Activision Blizzard owned three of the top fifteen–grossing mobile games for eight consecutive quarters":
Activision Blizzard. 2015 Annual Report. Web. 1 Dec 2016.

"Clash of Clans is developed by Supercell, a Finland-based studio":
http://supercell.com/en/our-story/

"Remarkably, Dong only tweeted marketing material once about Flappy Bird"; "Dong was earning an estimated $50,000 per day, and its success became a pop-culture sensation. Users directed fury and hatred toward the "evil" creator": Kushner, David. "Exclusive: Flappy Bird Creator Speaks." Rolling Stone. Rolling Stone, 11 Mar. 2014. Web.

"Inc's 5000 List of Fastest Growing Private Companies in the United States during 2016": https://www.inc.com/inc5000/list/2016/

"buzzword for anything posing as trendy and new."; Thiel believes those who say they are disrupters "see themselves through older firms' eyes.":
Theil, Peter, and Blake Masters. Zero to One: Notes on Startups, or How to Build the Future. New York: Crown Business, 2014. Print.

Chapter 5

TouchZen: http://www.touchzenmedia.com/

Chapter 7

NOTES

"It was once the most downloaded free apps in the iOS App Store": Souppouris, Aaron. "Vine Is Now the Number One Free App in the US App Store." The Verge. The Verge, 09 Apr. 2013. Web.

"By 2014, it had more than 40 million users": Blagdon, Jeff. "Vine Hits 40 Million Registered Users, but How Many Are Active?" The Verge. The Verge, 20 Aug. 2013. Web.

"Brittany Furlan, spent ten years in Hollywood chasing fame but became an overnight celebrity on Vine"; *"At one point, Furlan was earning between $7,000 and $20,000 per six-second clip"*: Gilman, Greg. "How Vine's Biggest Female Star Brittany Furlan Is Building a Career." TheWrap. N.p., 04 Aug. 2014. Web.

"North Carolina named Nash Grier became the most famous Vine celebrity in the world after amassing more than 12.7 million Vine followers addicted to his comedic content": Bosker, Bianca. "16 And Famous: How Nash Grier Became the Most Popular Kid In The World." The Huffington Post. TheHuffingtonPost.com, 07 Aug. 2014. Web.

"Over a hundred million people per month were watching Vine videos": Loren, Taylor. "With Its Latest Update, Vine Comes of Age (While Users Still Haven't)." Hootsuite Social Media Management. N.p., 22 Aug. 2014. Web.

"Burberry, General Electric, Coca-Cola, and other household name brands were rushing to establish a presence on the social media platform": Delo, Cotton. "10 Early-Adopter Brands That Are First to Try New Technology." Ad Age. N.p., 01 Aug. 2013. Web.

"Vine was acquired by Twitter in 2012 for a reported $30 million": Kharpal, Arjun. "'Don't Sell Your Company': Vine Founder's Advice as Pornhub Offers to Buy Axed App." CNBC. CNBC, 28 Oct. 2016. Web.

"In an attempt to capitalize on lost ground, Twitter purchased Niche, an agency that works with social media creators and brands to create meaningful content": Ha, Anthony. "Twitter Acquires Niche, A Startup That Helps Advertisers Work With Social Media Celebrities." TechCrunch. TechCrunch, 11 Feb. 2015. Web.

"Vine stars collectively walked away from the platform in 2016": Lorenz, Taylor. "'We Knew Vine Was Dead' - Vine's Biggest Stars Tried to save

the Company, but They Were Ignored." Business Insider. Business Insider, 29 Oct. 2016. Web.

"Twitter describes itself as "a global platform for public self-expression and conversation in real-time.": Guglielmo, Connie. "The Twitter IPO: 20 Talking Points." Forbes. Forbes Magazine, 12 Nov. 2013. Web.

"Twitter is a successful public company that earned over $2.5 billion in revenue during 2016": Twitter. Annual Report 2017. Web.

"Candy Crush Saga is notable for having tremendous success with in-app purchases. Users have purchased more than $1.3 billion of in-app content": Dredge, Stuart. "Candy Crush Saga Players Spent £865m on the Game in 2014 Alone." The Guardian. Guardian News and Media, 13 Feb. 2015. Web.

"According to the App Store website, 'users can buy in-app purchases to access content, services, and experiences for renewable or non-renewing durations'.": Apple. "Choosing a Business Model." Choosing a Business Model. N.p., n.d. Web. <https://developer.apple.com/app-store/business-models/>.

"During the first quarter of 2016... SensorTower estimated $1.34 billion of the projected $1.43 billion in sales went to only 623 publishers": Leswing, Kif. "The Top 1% of Developers Completely Dominates the App Store." Business Insider. Business Insider, 10 May 2016. Web.

"The remaining $86 million was spread among nearly 67,000 publishers.": Nelson, Randy. "Randy Nelson." 94% of U.S. App Store Revenue Comes From the Top 1% of Monetizing Publishers. N.p., 10 May 2016. Web.

CHAPTER 8

"a set of software that provides the infrastructure for a computer.": "Encyclopedia." PC Magazine. N.p., n.d. Web.

"Acquired by Facebook for $85 million during 2013": Rodriguez, Salvador. "Facebook Acquires Parse, an App-support Company, for $85 Million." Los Angeles Times. Los Angeles Times, 26 Apr. 2013. Web.

"Reportedly, Parse powered over 600,000 apps": Lardinois, Frederic, and Josh Constine. "Facebook Shutters Its Parse Developer Platform." TechCrunch. TechCrunch, 28 Jan. 2016. Web.

"Facebook would shut down Parse in January 2017": Weinberger, Matt. "Facebook Is Shutting down Parse, Its Effort to Take on Amazon's Cloud Supremacy." Business Insider. Business Insider, 28 Jan. 2016. Web.

CHAPTER 10

"The Wabash Lights project hopes to transform the L infrastructure on Wabash Avenue 'into a canvas for dynamic, interactive experience'.": Dallke, Jim. "This Kickstarter Wants to Put a Light Show Underneath Chicago's L Tracks." Chicago Inno. N.p., 25 June 2015. Web.
"Tech Giants Are Racing to Be the First to Develop 'The Last App'": Stecher, Benjamin. "Tech Giants Are Racing to Be the First to Develop." Futurism. N.p., 29 Mar. 2017. Web.

Michio Kaku, a theoretical physicist and best-selling author, often speaks about "The Caveman Principle.": Kaku, Michio. Physics of the Future: How Science Will Shape Human Destiny and Our Daily Lives by the Year 2100. New York: Anchor, 2012. Print.

www.ingramcontent.com/pod-product-compliance
Lightning Source LLC
Chambersburg PA
CBHW061440180526
45170CB00004B/1486